A Guide to the
Scottish Parliament

Edited by Gerry Hassan **with a foreword by** Rt Hon Donald Dewar

THE SHAPE
OF THINGS TO COME

The Centre for Scottish Public Policy is an independent centre-left think-tank established in 1990 which aims to further public policy debate via a range of activities such as conferences, seminars, research and publications. It aims to develop Scottish based solutions to Scottish policy issues. In all its work, the Centre brings together people from a wide range of expertise to share and cross-fertilise ideas and experiences and improve the quality and range of public policy debate.

The Centre is Scotland's only membership based public policy institute, with both individual and corporate membership. For further details about the Centre, its work and membership please contact:

Centre for Scottish Public Policy
20 Forth Street
Edinburgh EH1 3LH

Tel: 0131 477 8219
Tel/Fax: 0131 477 8220
email: mail@jwcentre.demon.co.uk

© The Stationery Office Limited 1999

The Stationery Office Limited
South Gyle Crescent
Edinburgh EH12 9EB

Applications for reproduction should be made to The Stationery Office Limited

First Published 1999

British Library Cataloguing in Publication Data
A Catalogue record of this book is available from the British Library

ISBN 01 1497 2311

Contents

The Shape of **Things to Come**

3

List of Tables and Figures

Contributors

Morag Alexander is Director of the Equal Opportunities Commission (Scotland).

Michael Bennett, Scottish Local Authorities Management Centre, Strathclyde University.

Alice Brown is Professor, Department of Politics, University of Edinburgh.

Andrew Burns is Secretary of Charter 88 Scotland.

Noreen Burrows is Professor, School of Law, University of Glasgow.

Gerry Hassan is Director of the Centre for Scottish Public Policy.

Brian Hogwood is Professor, Department of Government, Strathclyde University.

Mark McAteer, Scottish Local Authorities Management Centre, Strathclyde University.

Barry McCloud, Scottish Local Authorities Management Centre, Strathclyde University.

Robert McLean, author of 'Labour and Scottish Home Rule.'

Colin Mair, Scottish Local Authorities Management Centre, Strathclyde University.

Stephen Maxwell is Assistant Director, Scottish Council for Voluntary Organisations (SCVO).

James Mitchell is Professor, Department of Politics, Sheffield University.

Michelle Mitchell is Parliamentary Officer, Charter 88.

Andy Myles is Scottish Parliamentary Officer, Royal Society for the Protection of Birds.

Sarah O'Neill is Legal Adviser of the Scottish Consumer Council.

Richard Parry is lecturer at the Department of Social Policy, University of Edinburgh.

Joan Stringer is Principal of Queen Margaret College, Edinburgh.

Acknowledgements

A project such as this has been brought together through the contributions, support and advice of numerous people. It has been made possible by the long-term research work and priorities of the Centre for Scottish Public Policy and the support and encouragement of The Stationery Office.

I would like to take this opportunity to thank each and every one of the contributors for being so supportive of this project and eager to deliver text and amendments to what seemed impossible deadlines.

In particular, I thank Alice Brown, Head of Politics, University of Edinburgh, who read over drafts of each section, Pat Herd and Amy Jones of the Centre for Scottish Public Policy, who proofed each section and tirelessly checked and rechecked facts and figures and Rosemary Ilett, who oversaw the final proofs and edits with humour and patience.

Finally, I would like to show my appreciation to Gillian Stirton at The Stationery Office for supporting this project.

In closing, I dedicate this publication to my mother, Jean Grieg, who for as long as the debate about a Scottish Parliament has raged back and forward has remained a staunch sceptic of the whole project. I hope that this publication might help her to finally see what all the fuss is about and what some of us have spent many years of our lives trying to bring about.

Gerry Hassan
Director
Centre for Scottish Public Policy
February 1999

Foreword by the Secretary of State for Scotland

This is an historic year for Scotland - the end of one era and the beginning of a new one defined by opportunity, optimism and looking to the future.

The establishment of a Scottish Parliament offers us the prospect of building a new kind of Scotland with modern, relevant, open and of transparent government. It allows us the chance to make a new politics more at home with pluralism, inclusiveness and co-operation than the old, outdated adversarial structures, a politics more in tune with Scottish needs and opinions - of solutions and policies made in and for Scotland.

The people of Scotland rightly have high hopes and expectations for their Parliament; they already feel a sense of ownership and of connection to it and we must not let them down. Across a range of policy areas, health, education, housing and social policy, people believe that the Parliamentwill make a positive contribution.

This process of change cannot be brought about by politicians alone, but must involve people the length and breadth of Scotland getting involved in the life of their communities and feeling that they can make a difference. The Scottish Parliament allows us the opportunity to nurture a vision of a new, fairer Scotland where the current generation of young Scots can grow up with choices previous generations could only dream of making in Scotland.

This is why a publication such as 'A Guide to The Scottish Parliament: The Shape of Things to Come' published under the auspices of the Centre for Scottish Public Policy is so important in this exciting year.

The Scottish Parliament does not in itself banish the difficult choices and dilemmas which are at the heart of politics. It will, however, allow those decisions to be made closer to home by those it will affect. It will reconnect people with politics and bring a new sense of ownership and belonging to the public life of Scotland.

Scotland stands at the beginning of a new era, a new century and a new millennium. We have it within our power to make sure that the next period in Scotland's history is defined by what is best about Scotland. And that means instead of turning inward and emphasising the past, we should focus outward to the wider world and the challenges of the future. Scotland has within its rich traditions the diversity, cosmopolitan nature and sense of itself, for us to be sure that the future will be one where the best of Scotland is yet to come.

Rt. Hon Donald Dewar
Secretary of State for Scotland

Chapter One:
The New Scottish Politics

Gerry Hassan

The Establishment of a Scottish Parliament

The countdown is on to the first Scottish Parliamentary elections in over 300 years - the first ever democratic Scottish Parliament elections.

The pace of change has been at times bewildering. From the election of a Labour Government in May 1997 to the first elections in May 1999 will only be just over two years. The Scotland Act was published as a Bill on December 17th 1997 and received Royal Assent on November 19th 1998. It was debated for 191 hours and 43 minutes in Parliament totalling 32 days of Westminster debate - 15 in the Commons and 17 in the Lords. In total, 2,025 amendments were tabled - 670 by the Government. (1)

What these figures do not reveal is that this Scotland Act had a much more smooth journey through the Commons and Lords than the previous Scotland Act. This began as the Scotland and Wales Bill 1976, and had to be separated into the Scotland Act 1978 and Wales Act 1978 due to the strength of anti-devolution opinion in the then Labour Government's ranks and its lack of an overall majority during the 1976-79 period. The Labour Party then had to concede referendums as part of a reactive strategy to limit opposition in its own ranks, whereas this time the Labour leadership boldly announced their intention to hold referendums even before Labour entered office.

The difference between then and now is more fundamental than that. In the 1970s, the Labour Government and wider political circles were not persuaded of the merits of devolution, but came around to championing them for reasons of political expediency and

The Shape of **Things to Come**

9

in particular, the perceived electoral threat of Plaid Cymru and more fundamentally, the SNP. Labour's devolution proposals then were in part driven by the centre's concern over the nationalist threat.

Henry Drucker and Gordon Brown acknowledged this at the time:

> *'Devolution must be taken out of the relatively restricted confines of Scotland and Wales and seen as part of an attempt to make British government more acceptable to the British people ....'* (2)

Today, the situation has radically altered. The devolution proposals which the Government has implemented for Scotland and Wales are much more home based and designed than was previously the case, yet they also fit into part of a wider package of constitutional reforms which is radically altering the governance of the United Kingdom.

Table One: Timetable of Events

November 30 1995	Publication of Scottish Constitution Convention report 'Scotland's Parliament, Scotland's Right'
June 26 1996	Blair announces two question referendum for Scotland
May 1 1997	Labour Government elected
May 15 1997	Referendums (Scotland and Wales) Bill published
July 24 1997	'Scotland's Parliament' White Paper published
July 31 1997	Referendums (Scotland and Wales) Act receives Royal Assent
September 11 1997	Scottish referendum gives emphatic majorities to both questions
December 17 1997	Scotland Bill published
January 13 1998	Consultative Steering Group set up
November 19 1998	Scotland Act receives Royal Assent
January 15 1999	'Shaping Scotland's Parliament' Consultative Steering Group report published

Table Two: Future Timetable of Events

April 5 1999	Probable start of Scottish election campaign
May 6 1999	First Scottish Parliamentary elections
May 12 1999	First meeting of Scottish Parliament and election of Presiding Officer (and deputies)
May 13 1999	Second meeting of Scottish Parliament - nomination of First Minister
May 28 1999	Last date for election of First Minister
By end of May 1999	Formation of first Scottish Executive and Government
July 1 1999	Official opening of Scottish Parliament: beginning of transfer of powers from UK Government
Summer 1999	Parliamentary recess
Autumn 1999	Parliamentary committee structure put in place
Early 2000	Scottish Parliament takes full powers
May 2003	Second Scottish Parliament elections

The Scottish Policy-Making Environment

Scotland has enjoyed a degree of autonomy and distinctiveness in its institutional arrangements within the United Kingdom from the Treaty of Union in 1707 onwards. There is much debate and disagreement among commentators and observers about the extent of the autonomy Scotland has been able to practice in the pre-devolution era.

At one end of the spectrum, taking a maximalist view of autonomy, James Kellas has observed a 'Scottish political system' which 'does justice to the scale and nature of the phenomena which are found in Scottish politics' (3). At the other more minimalist end, Midwinter, Keating and Mitchell have argued:

'There is a British political system which is periodically under stress in Scotland .... The Scottish environment and civil society places specific demands on British government, which is forced to produce responses which may be differentiated yet which maintain the integrity of the British system as a whole.' (4)

The nature of Scottish autonomy is in Lindsay Paterson's words 'managed' and 'partial.' (5) Rooted in the distinctiveness of Scots civil society, its radicalism has been blunted by the institutional incorporation of various groups and elites. Paterson views its capacity for innovation and creation, which once fed into and sustained Scottish autonomy, as having become exhausted by the 1960s. (6) It will be up to the Scottish policy communities and those involved in public policy debates to show that the Scots capacity for imagination and innovation has not been lost.

The Wider Policy Environment

What constitutes Scottish politics in the United Kingdom has never been clear-cut or easy to define. The Scottish Parliament will change this - remaking and redefining Scottish politics and a Scottish political system which will become more distinctive, autonomous and self-confident.

The Scottish Parliament arrives at a point where we have witnessed a fundamental and far-reaching transformation in what we think of and understand as politics, policy and political processes. The concept and practice of policy has been radically transformed in the last 20-30 years. Firstly, traditional mechanisms of policy-making have declined and been increasingly challenged and sidelined. The old policy elites of the civil service, universities and political parties no longer have the same influence, status and respect in policy discussions that they once had.

The civil service have become a product of the Thatcherisation of many of the institutions of British public life - with their size and status diluted and their scope for creative policy formulation diminished.

Academics have become increasingly specialised and distanced from public policy debates, while political parties have become bureaucratised and professionalised - more vehicles for career advancement, than ideological commitment, and more reliant on the politics of image and spin than substance.

The crisis of government and politics which has prevailed in the West for the last twenty-five years is inter-twined with a crisis of public agency and traditional political philosophies, making the means and ends of policy-making more problematic.

This retreat from politics is mirrored by a widespread disillusion with politicians, aptly described by the German writer Hans Magnus Enzenberger, quoted with approval by Anthony Giddens in his recent 'The Third Way':

> 'The politicians are insulted that people are less and less interested in them ... [but] innovations and decisions on the future have not originated from the political class for some time now ... The [German] Federal Government is relatively stable and relatively successful, despite and not because of the fact that it is ruled by those people grinning down at us from the campaign posters .... Germany can afford an incompetent government, because ultimately the people who bore us in the daily news really do not matter.' (7)

The challenge to the Scottish Parliament will be to tackle the manifestation of this global trend in Scotland which sees politics and politicians as irrelevant to the problems of everyday life.

A New Policy-Making Culture

Scottish policy has previously been shaped by a small group of senior Ministers and civil servants at the Scottish Office with the minimum degree of democratic scrutiny and debate. If they have had the vision and determination to see a policy from inception to implementation they have been able to put it onto the statute book and into practice.

The election of a Labour Government in May 1997 saw a change of ethos in the Scottish Office, with a new emphasis on openness, consultation and a flexible, evolving agenda. However, Scottish Office senior ministers also underlined the immense challenges and constraints on the horizon - of pressures and demands on the Scottish Office £14 billion budget and the pent-up nature of expectations across Scottish opinion after 18 years of Conservative Government.

Transforming the Scottish Office culture of conservatism and caution to one which champions and nurtures innovation and forward-thinking will only happen slowly and requires more than a change of government and ministers. It requires more than the establishment of a Scottish Parliament, needing deep-seated organisational and cultural change at every level of Scottish life.

The process of developing a new approach to policy-making will involve engaging with the policy-making community across Scotland and reaching out beyond those already well represented in established channels of power, to include smaller organisations at national, regional and local level.

The Scottish Parliament has to consider different models of representation which go beyond the significant players of corporate and established Scotland: the private sector, trade unions and large voluntary organisations. New formats of consultation and involvement have to be devised which go beyond the old top-down Parliamentary model of committee representation. The Consultative Steering Group (8) has made an auspicious start here, but this need for new forms of governance will require bold and imaginative thinking beyond Scotland's political classes.

A New Approach to Policy-Making

The Scottish Parliament must foster a new policy agenda which addresses Scottish distinctiveness and difference with policies and prescriptions relevant to our needs. A second part of the equation will be to develop policy and ideas in this framework which embrace pluralism and innovation, rather than conservatism and stasis.

Already all the political parties are re-branding themselves - positioning themselves as 'Scotland's party', emphasising their credentials as Scottish, or stressing the home based nature of their policy-making with a programme 'made in Scotland.' A classic example of this new politics of Scottish positioning can be found in claims by Alex Salmond, the SNP leader, in the recent 'Scotsman' debate:

> 'We are Scotland's party. We will act in Scotland's Parliament. The SNP will not take instructions from anyone else bar the Scottish people.' (9)

All the major political parties have produced Scottish manifestos for British general elections for over twenty years, but these have often been - with the exception of the SNP - nothing more than Scottish revisions of British based manifestos and priorities. From now on, the parties will have to develop policy and research networks previously uncalled for, to draw up detailed policy prospectuses for Scottish circumstances and consumption.

The Consultative Steering Group has made a number of recommendations on the committee structure for the new Parliament. It envisages nine committees, but does not intend this to be prescriptive, and does not venture forth on the nature of most of the Subject Committees. (10)

It is however, clear at the moment that with a 129 member Parliament there is a limit to the number of Subject Committees due to the size of the Executive, Government payroll vote and the actual number of backbench MSPs available to serve on them. This has consequences for addressing policy areas. Instead of the compartmentalisation of Westminster and Whitehall, a more thematic and cross-disciplinary approach to policy will be required. This will involve committees addressing policy in a more integrated way, for example, by health and housing being combined, and education and training.

A New Framework for A New Policy

Richard Parry has observed that 'devolution is less a search for policy development than an expression of political identity and as such an unstable settlement'. (11) He identified three social policy futures for the Parliament which have a wider relevance as policy scenarios under devolution:

- 'PROFESSIONALLY-BASED STASIS':
  where the Scottish professional classes and elites use their influence to maintain their privilege and influence;

- 'CONFLICT-RIDDEN POLICY':
  where differences between expectations and the actual policy agenda of a Parliament shape public debate;

- 'INNOVATIVE POLICY':
  led by flexibility, innovation and client led policies. (12)

Although Parry does not state it, it is implicit in his analysis that he sees a Scottish Parliament as being more likely defined by the first two scenarios than the third innovative model. This is partly because at the moment there is still a lack of clarity about where the champions and advocates of this third way will emerge from, while it is all too clear that powerful interests will act as advocates of the first two options.

James Mitchell, borrowing from Ted Lowi, identifies the following policy categories which are helpful in understanding the context in which a Scottish Parliament will operate:

*   DISTRIBUTIVE POLICIES:
    'handouts to groups rather than individuals' such as farmers and local authorities;

*   REDISTRIBUTIVE POLICIES:
    'redistribution between classes of people' via taxation and social security;

*   REGULATORY POLICIES:
    'public control over private activities in the public interest' such as consumer and environmental protection';

*   PROCESS OF POLICY MAKING:
    procedures to take policies from 'agenda setting to implementation'. (13)

According to Mitchell, the Scottish Parliament will not have much room to develop redistributive policies with taxation and social security retained by central government. There will be more opportunities for distributive policies, but this will take time to develop as this area is characterised by the strength of interest and pressure groups and so is slow to effect change within.

Regulatory policies offer the Parliament one of the most hopeful areas to bring about change. An influential model here is the European Commission which with a small budget, staff and powers has found regulatory policy an inexpensive and efficient way of setting common standards over such areas as environmental and consumer protection and minimum standards of social rights.

Regulatory policies offer a potential model for the Scottish Parliament. At one level, they do not involve Government directly running services or setting up new bureaucracies and expenditures, but involve them in setting agreed rules which are then implemented by other agencies. Active government can then be linked with the politics of decentralism. Regulatory policies are thus an appropriate vision of government in an age where on one level the state is under attack and critique, yet more and more is expected from it by the general public.

It also contains within it the prospect of engaging with the realities and pressures of multi-layered governance and the emergence of a complex nexus of relationships between different institutions which cannot be characterised simply as a hierarchy of different levels of government from local government to the European Union. (14)

The First Scottish Parliamentary Elections

The outcome of the first Scottish Parliament elections on May 6th 1999 will be extremely difficult to predict for two main reasons. The first is the new electoral system (described in further detail in Chapter Eleven) where voters will have two votes, with every opinion poll so far indicating a significant difference in voting behaviour between the two, and movement between first and second votes.

The second is the emergence of new voting patterns for the new Parliament. Scottish politics has been characterised for the last forty years by an asymmetrical system of one-party dominance in favour of the Labour Party which now may be changing. This dominance has never been as all-encompassing as it has sometimes seemed - based more on the distortions of the First Past the Post (FPTP) electoral system than Labour's real strength; in the 1997 general election Labour won with 46% of the vote and 78% of the seats.

The voting patterns in Tables Three and Four show that Scotland may be shifting to a two party competitive system where the principal contest is between Labour and SNP. If the first Scottish Parliamentary elections are characterised by this kind of contest it will mark a new era of Scottish politics and one that will require all political parties to develop new strategies.

This new era of politics will be aided by the likelihood (shown in Table Five) that no political party on its own will win an overall majority in the new Parliament, requiring agreements to be reached between parties on an issue by issue basis and the possibility of a coalition administration between more than one party.

Table Three: Scottish Parliament First Vote Intentions

	Scotsman/ ICM	Herald/ System Three	Herald Sunday/ MORI
Fieldwork	31/1-2/2	28/1-2/2	10-11/2
Sample Size	1,009	1,017	1,000
Labour	44	41	43
SNP	32	39	38
Conservative	12	9	9
Liberal Democrat	10	10	9

Table Four: Scottish Parliament Second Vote Intentions

Labour	39	38	39
SNP	34	38	37
Conservative	13	13	10
Liberal Democrat	11	10	12

Table Five: Possible Composition of Scottish Parliament

Labour	57	57	56
SNP	43	46	49
Conservative	16	9	9
Liberal Democrat	13	17	15

The Future of Scottish Politics

The Scottish people have high expectations of the Parliament on a variety of policy issues, with between two-thirds to three-quarters of people expecting it to improve education, health, social welfare and the economy, and only small minorities expecting matters to get worse. (15) The Parliament's inheritance will be this high degree of support and goodwill, and the challenge will be not to disillusion, but capture the imagination of this public opinion.

It is the aim of this guide produced by the Centre for Scottish Public Policy, to offer a concise and easy to read, but comprehensive analysis and description of how the Parliament will work and its potential relations with wider society and other institutions. We have been fortunate in being able to bring together an impressive range of experts and writers across several different fields to put this guide together, and we hope that it will be a useful contribution to the democratic process of understanding where Scotland is at the moment and its potential future roads.

Chapter Two: A Brief History of Scottish Home Rule

Robert McLean

Since the incorporating union of Scotland with England in 1707 there has been a Scottish national/home rule movement of some sort. No sooner had the Act of Union been enacted than cries of betrayal and unfair treatment were heard.

However, it is to the 1880s that we have to look for the birth of the modern Scottish home rule movement. It was a key decade in the shaping of modern Scotland, as the second Industrial Revolution carved out something resembling the map of today's Scotland (1). The labour demanded by the growth of heavy industries was met by rural migration and Irish immigration. (2) The prospects for political reform were greatly enhanced by the third Reform Act of 1884, which extended the franchise to the male heads of all households. While all women, and many working-class men, continued to be denied the vote, it was possible from that point on to talk of a mass working-class electorate. Throughout the decade the Liberal Leader, William Gladstone, battled to accommodate the demands of the Irish national and land movements, and an increasingly powerful trade union movement which was growing restive with the practice of seeking political representation through the Liberal Party.

The First Labour Party

Across the Highlands and Islands of Scotland tenant farmers were in revolt against their landlords. This took the form of civil disobedience and the development of an independent political organisation which called for the establishment of a Scottish Parliament to redress wrongs. The 'Crofters' MPs', those elected with the support of the Highland Land League in 1885 and 1886, were the first independent working-class representatives to take their seats at Westminster. The Crofters had been encouraged by the influence wielded by the nationalist Irish Parliamentary Party, and sought to do the same. They were led by Dr. Gavin B. Clark, a London-based Scottish doctor, who, prior to being elected to represent the crofters of Caithness, had been a member of the Executive of the International Working Men's Association, the 'First International'. In that capacity he had come to

know and admire Karl Marx. Later, he would go on to become a
founding member of both the Scottish Home Rule Association and
the Scottish Labour Party.

The Scottish Home Rule Association

London responded to Highland demands with a Royal Commission
on the land and the inclusion of a Secretary of State for Scotland in
the British Cabinet. (3) This success encouraged the formation of the
first Scottish Home Rule Association (SHRA) in 1886. Unlike the
Crofters and the Irish Nationalists, the Association did not seek to
field candidates of its own but to lobby MPs and political aspirants,
regardless of party. In 1888 the SHRA supported the candidature of
one of its Vice Presidents, James Keir Hardie, when he contested a
by-election in the Mid-Lanark division, an event that would change
the course of Scottish history.

Mid-Lanark and the Scottish Labour Party

Rebuffed by the local Liberal Association, miners' union official Keir
Hardie decided to contest the by-election as an independent Labour
candidate. His candidature was supported by an alliance of local trade
unions, Crofters, Scottish Home Rulers, dissident Irish Nationalists, and
individual Radical Liberals, including the flamboyant MP R.B.
Cunninghame Graham. The national leaderships of trade unions and
the Irish National League, the grass roots organisation working among
the Irish Catholic community in Scotland, remained loyal to the Liberal
Party. Hardie's platform contained a clear and prominent commitment
to Scottish Home Rule. Although he polled only 8% of the vote the
mould was broken, and the Scottish party system would never be the
same again. Later in 1888, the Mid-Lanark Alliance reconvened in
Glasgow and, with Cunninghame Graham as Chair, declared itself the
Scottish Labour Party (SLP). (4) The 'first' Scottish Labour Party
continued to 1893 when it became one of the components of the
British-wide Independent Labour Party. The perspective of the SLP was
important in ensuring that the early British Labour Party had a strong
commitment to Scottish Home Rule.

Home Rule All Round

Gladstone's support for Irish home rule split Liberal ranks in 1895
with the dissident minority styling themselves as Liberal Unionists. In

Scotland the breakaway Liberals merged with the Tories to form the Scottish Unionist Party, the name retained by Conservatives in Scotland until as recently as 1964. (5) Historical associations with Jacobitism and 'Landlordism' had left Toryism with little support in Scotland, but the union with the Liberal Unionists provided an anti-Irish home rule, working-class Protestant base which continued into the 1960s.

The Liberal response was 'home rule all round.' By advocating a federal future for the nations of the British Isles, Gladstone believed he could meet Irish aspirations yet minimise the mainland backlash by linking the Irish measure to home rule for Scotland and Wales. The policy was endorsed by the Scottish Liberal Association as a durable formula capable of delivering success, but its implementation was delayed by the outbreak of World War One, and undermined by events in Ireland. The success of Sinn Fein in nationalist Ireland in the British general election of 1918 effectively rendered the 'home rule all round' solution obsolete. The final attempt to find a common constitutional framework for the United Kingdom as a whole, the Speaker's Conference of 1919, was doomed to failure from the outset. (6)

Labour in Government

Events in Ireland had implications for the political allegiance of the Irish community in Scotland. The increasing irrelevance of 'home rule' to Irish national aspirations undermined community support for the Liberal Party, and some in the community looked towards political allies prepared to support independence for Ireland. Following the establishment of the Free State in 1921 those of Irish Catholic descent looked to Labour in greater numbers.

As Labour continued to eclipse the Liberals as the leading alternative to Unionism, the SHRA pinned its fate to an electoral breakthrough by Labour. Expectations were running high in 1923/24 when Labour formed a minority government. It fell to George Buchanan, MP for Glasgow Gorbals, to sponsor a Scottish home rule bill. Despite frontbench and Liberal support, the measure was talked out by the Unionist opposition amid riotous scenes. With the fall of the fragile Labour administration, the Home Rule Association opted for a different strategy. It would convene a Scottish National Convention with the remit of developing a broad consensus around a detailed scheme which would subsequently be put to Parliament.

The Scottish National Convention

The Scottish National Convention worked diligently for two years and involved 29 MPs, 28 local authorities and the Convention of Scottish Royal Burghs. The Rev. James Barr MP presented the Convention scheme to Parliament in May 1927, seconded by Tom Johnston. The Bill was talked out, as was a second attempt to introduce an amended version in 1928. The failure of the Buchanan and Barr bills led to major reassessment within the Scottish Home Rule Association and the wider national movement.

The Birth of the Scottish National Party

The debate within the SHRA was between forming an independent nationalist party or continuing to lobby within the existing party system. Those who argued for the latter maintained that the verdict on Labour's willingness to introduce home rule had to be deferred until such time as the party formed a majority government. The internal SHRA debate was not allowed to come to a conclusion and it was upstaged by John MacCormick. His Glasgow University Scottish Nationalist Association called a meeting of all those favouring the independent party strategy. The initiative was supported by veteran home rulers Roland Muirhead, the financial and organisational mainstay of the SHRA and Cunninghame Graham. Cunninghame Graham had chaired the inaugural meeting of the Scottish Labour Party in the summer of 1888 and exactly forty years later took the Chair at the inaugural meeting of the National Party of Scotland. Six years later the leftish-leaning National Party merged with the Tory breakaway Scottish Party to form the Scottish National Party. (7)

Tom Johnston at the Scottish Office

The creation of an independent nationalist party, structural changes in the British economy, reflected in trade union organisation, and the 'disaffiliation' of the Independent Labour Party contributed to a steady decline in Labour's interest in Scottish home rule, which would ultimately lead to outright opposition to the concept by 1958. The intervening war years, however, led to an unprecedented experiment in Scottish self-government. In an inspired move to bind Scotland and its Labour movement to the war effort, Churchill appointed Labour's Tom Johnston as Scottish Secretary in his coalition government. A former editor of the ILP's 'Forward', Johnston was an old-time Home Ruler. He had been a member of the SHRA, and had seconded both Buchanan's and Barr's home rule bills. Johnston accepted his appointment in return for freedom of action, and convened a Scottish Council of State comprised of all previous Scottish Secretaries. If there was consensus in the Council, there was no requirement to refer that particular legislation to Westminster. Taking full advantage of this, Johnston went on to lay much of the basis for the post-war reconstruction of Scotland. (8)

The National Covenant

With the ending of World War Two, and the election of the first majority Labour Government, Labour's interest in Scottish home rule continued to decline. Within the SNP there was soul searching as to whether or not the decision to create an independent nationalist party had brought the establishment of a Scottish Parliament any closer. Losing the argument for gradualism in the wartime SNP, John MacCormick, and his financial backer Roland Muirhead, formed the Scottish Convention, which in 1947 convened a Scottish National Assembly along similar lines to the Scottish National Convention of the 1920s. By the end of 1948 this cross party gathering has approved a 'blueprint' for a Scottish Parliament within the UK, and in October 1949 it launched a National Covenant, a monster petition, to demonstrate support for home rule. Fuelled by resentment against some of the centralising consequences of the post-war Labour Government actions, the Covenant gained two million signatures by 1952. The Covenant faltered in the face of Labour and Tory government intransigence, and by 1953 the campaign had run out of steam. It ushered in a decade of unchallenged Unionist hegemony. (9)

SNP Breakthrough

The 'you've never had it so good' era drew to an end in Scotland in the early 1960s. The Tories, who achieved their highest ever share of the Scottish vote in 1955, started on a terminal decline, propelled by social changes, including a decrease in religious-based voting. Harold Wilson's Labour Government ran into early trouble in Scotland as the collapse of its economic policy led to closures and unemployment in Scotland's heavy industries, and a contraction of services in rural Scotland. The Glasgow Bridgeton and West Lothian by-elections of 1961 and 1962 demonstrated the SNP's potential to emerge from the political fringe. The breakthrough to the mainstream came in 1967/68 with 28% in the Glasgow Pollok by-election, Winnie Ewing's victory at Hamilton and a net gain of 103 seats in the municipal elections of May 1968. Ted Heath hurried to Perth to declare that devolution was on the Tory agenda after all, and Harold Wilson established the Royal Commission on the Constitution. These initiatives seemed to have bought political space but by February 1974 Labour was back in office but without a majority, and the SNP returned seven MPs. The summer of 1974 saw the enforced conversion of Scottish Labour's ranks to the old home rule faith. In October 1974 the SNP increased its representation to eleven but exclusively at the expense of the Tories. Wilson sneaked back into Downing Street with the narrowest of majorities.

The Referendum Experience

The Labour Government's efforts to legislate for a Scottish Assembly, from October 1974 to the referendum of March 1st 1979, is outwith the scope of this summary. (10) The political snakes and ladders played at Westminster during those years was reminiscent of Gladstone's dealings with Parnell in the 1880s. For both premiers the delivery of some form of home rule was essential to sustaining their majorities but they had to manage opposition and agnosticism in their own ranks.

The tenor of those times is encapsulated in Helen Liddell's remark, at the press launch of the 'Labour Movement Yes Campaign', that the Labour Party would not 'soil its hands' in working with other parties to achieve a majority for the Assembly. (11)

One attempt to forge cross-party co-operation was Yes For Scotland, which drew together Liberals, the breakaway Scottish Labour Party led by Jim Sillars, Communists, non-aligned activists, and even a few pro-devolution Tories. It was largely ignored by the Labour Party while active SNP involvement varied from area to area. The Labour Movement Campaign was neutered by divisions in the party over the issue. Meanwhile the linkage between a Yes victory and the survival of the Labour Government created a dilemma for non-Labour Scotland.

While there were as many No campaigns as Yes campaigns, the anti-devolutionists were able to forge a more effective unity in action.

While 62.8% of the Scottish people turned out, and a clear majority (51.6%) of those who voted cast a Yes preference, the pro-Assembly votes amounted to 32.9% of the registered Scottish electorate, thereby, falling foul of the peculiar 40% device. (12)

The Campaign for a Scottish Parliament and the Convention Strategy

The failure of the referendum, and the election two months later of the resolutely Unionist Thatcher Conservative Government, marked a nadir in the fortunes of the home rule cause, but from those same ashes new organisations and a new phase in the campaign emerged. On the first anniversary of the referendum the remnants of Yes For Scotland crammed into the Edinburgh Trades Council Club to form the Campaign for a Scottish Assembly (CSA - later re-named the Campaign for a Scottish Parliament) with the aim of securing 'a Scottish Assembly, or Parliament, with such powers as desired by the Scottish people'. The first strategy paper presented to the organisation called for the convening of a 'National Convention'. Isobel Lindsay, then a leading figure in the SNP, told the inaugural meeting that the job of the Convention would be to 'work out what the Scots really want', and that she was prepared to concede that it might not equate with her preferred constitutional solution. (13)

The 'Doomsday Scenario'

The case for a Scottish Parliament gained few media headlines in the early 1980s, but was revived by the results of the 1983, and particularly the 1987, general elections. The result of the June 1987 general election was consistent with the trend that had developed from 1959 onwards. While Thatcher's Tories won more than twice the number of seats captured by Labour in the rest of the United Kingdom, in Scotland Labour returned 50 MPs to the Tories derisory 10. The much discussed 'Doomsday Scenario', of Tory victory in the UK but a Tory rout in Scotland, had been translated into reality. The Tories were rocked but the result also posed problems for the Donald Dewar-led Scottish Labour as to how the Party responded to its resounding mandate.

The Claim of Right and the Scottish Constitutional Convention

In an attempt to jump-start the Campaign for a Scottish Assembly's Convention strategy, senior civil servant turned home rule campaigner, Jim Ross, proposed in November 1987 that the CSA should invite a group of prominent and respected Scots to join a Constitutional Steering Committee to report on the theoretical basis and possible composition of a Convention. (14) With Sir Robert Grieve as chair, and Jim Ross as secretary, the Steering Committee concluded its remit with the publication of 'A Claim of Right for Scotland' in July 1988. The Claim was the basis for an historic meeting of Scotland's political leaders (all except the boycotting Tories) in January 1989. This gathering seized the attention of the international media, and for a few days it appeared as if the widest range of pro-Scottish Parliament opinion would be represented in the proposed Convention.

The SNP, however, decided not to participate, and the first meeting of the Scottish Constitutional Convention convened without them in March 1989. Present were Labour, the Liberal Democrats, minority political parties, trade unions, the churches, local government and other civic organisations. Despite doubts that such a varied grouping could achieve a consensus, the Constitutional Convention published two blueprints for the establishment of a Scottish Parliament within the United Kingdom, 'Towards Scotland's Parliament' in 1990, and the more detailed 'Scotland's Parliament, Scotland's Right' on St Andrew's Day 1995.

The Impact of the Convention on Scotland's Political Culture

There is little doubt that participation in the Scottish Constitutional Convention, like the Royal Commission twenty years earlier, bought political space for Scottish Labour in the years between the 'Doomsday' election of 1987 and its British victory in 1997. (15) Participation in the Convention, however, has left its impact on the culture and policies of the Party. Participation was a reversal of Labour's opposition to cross-party co-operation, as was the Party's agreement to the introduction of proportional representation, in the form of the Additional Members System, for elections to the Scottish Parliament. The dropping of the term 'Assembly', in favour of

'Parliament', was an indication that the 1990s proposals would empower the Scottish legislature with a wider range of powers than those proposed in the 1970s, including an element of discretion in revenue raising.

Involvement in the Convention contributed to the culture which enabled effective cross-party co-operation under the banner of Scotland Forward in the referendum of September 1997, the final act which entrenched the establishment of Scotland's Parliament in the votes of the people.

Chapter Three:
Scotland's Parliament White Paper

Andy Myles

After the election of the New Labour Government in May 1997, the Scottish Office went into overdrive to produce a White Paper stating their policy for the Parliament. By the beginning of July the paper, 'Scotland's Parliament', was ready, presented to the Commons and launched at a reception in the Great Hall of Edinburgh Castle. Donald Dewar commented at the time :

'In my time I have seen many devolution schemes. I genuinely believe this is the best and right for Scotland. We have renewed, modernised and improved on the plans agreed within the broad coalition of Scotish interests in the Scottish Constitutional Convention. It will provide a new, stable settlement, which will serve Scotland and the UK well in years to come'. (1)

Several factors intervened, however, to alter the Convention blueprint and turn it into the White Paper. The first was civil service advice as to the best way to deliver the Convention's promise. The Convention had worked for an agreed framework. The Scottish Office filled in the details of delivery, providing, for example, the mechanism by which the agreed tax-varying powers might be implemented. A second factor was the 'Unionism' of several members of the Cabinet, expressed in a variety of ways during the process of drawing up the White Paper in Whitehall. Several Cabinet members represented the strong Labour tradition of support for the Union that constitutes the United Kingdom and argued to limit powers of the proposed Parliament, by insisting on the vigorous assertion of the theory of the supremacy of 'the Crown in Parliament' - that being the Westminster Parliament. A third factor was an element of retreat from the Convention scheme, which can be seen as the high water mark of Labour's commitment to Home Rule. The White Paper described the Parliament as making the Scottish Office accountable for the exercise of its functions, but also conceded that those functions and powers were to be increased. The Convention document started from the Claim of Right and first principles rather than this more limited approach of merely amending the existing structure. A fourth factor was the need to fill minor gaps left by the Convention, which had not, for example, dealt with the intricacies of powers over subordinate legislation.

It is not feasible to ascertain which of these affected the process of drawing up the White Paper most, or at which specific point, but each of the factors had a mildly corrosive effect in the transformation of 'Scotland's Parliament, Scotland's Right' into 'Scotland's Parliament'.

The fear of the legislation becoming bogged down at Westminster in complex arguments over lists of powers, as had happened to the Scotland Bill in 1977 and 1978, had lead to the adoption of the 'reserved powers' model in the White Paper. The powers listed in the new Bill would be those reserved for Westminster and all else would be the responsibility of the new Parliament. This had been argued for in the Convention by many participants, and its adoption by Labour was fairly positively received. Nevertheless, there were signs of ministerial tussles in the list of reserved powers.

Jack Straw, painted as the arch 'Unionist', was reported to have demanded the reservation of drug and firearm laws, and these were found on the reserved list where it had been assumed they would be devolved. Some eyebrows were raised in Scotland at the weakness of the commitment to powers for the Parliament in the field of equal opportunities, which the Convention had agreed were to be devolved. Concern was quietly voiced, similarly, at the lack of devolved powers over broadcasting and competition policy. Overall there was a sense of retreat over the extent of the devolved powers. This was only partially mitigated by the mention of sensibly flexible arrangements for the possibility of further transfers from and to the list of reserved powers - effectively by mutual consent of the Westminster and Scottish institutions. Compared to 1978 though, the Parliament would have powers over economic development, financial and other assistance to industry, universities, training, forestry, certain transport matters and the police and prosecution system, which the Assembly would not have had.

Where the audience for the Convention's blueprint had been largely the Scottish public, the White Paper showed signs of being written for Westminster as well. The new constitutional arrangements were described to leave no doubt that this was to be power devolved and power retained. Heavy emphasis was placed on the absolute sovereignty of Westminster and all mention dropped of the Convention's agreed Solemn Declaration by Lords and Commons that the consent of the Scottish people would be required before any abolition or reduction in the powers of the Scottish Parliament.

Where the Convention had carefully agreed that the Parliament would start with Westminster's boundaries, it had also agreed that these would be replaced in time to protect the 129 number of MSPs, which was to be a minimum. In the White Paper this had disappeared and been replaced by the statement that 'The integrity of the UK will be strengthened by common parliamentary boundaries' (2), a change later to cause some of the few bitter exchanges between the Convention partners in Westminster debates on the Bill. The boundary issues were exacerbated by one of the White Paper additions to the Convention scheme, namely the decision that, in time the number of Scottish Westminster MPs would be reduced to a level proportionate with Scotland's population. This was only partially mitigated by the recognition that the ratio of constituency and additional members be maintained - and thus the proportionality of the electoral system protected.

The European Union and Scotland's role in international relations were given much greater prominence and amplification in the White Paper than had been the case within the Convention. The Government spelt out the mechanisms whereby the new Scottish Executive and Parliament would be involved in UK delegations and able to speak on behalf of the UK in international arenas within an agreed UK position. 'Scotland's Parliament' detailed the appointments to European institutions which would be made by the new Scottish Executive. One of the Convention's main borrowings from Europe had quietly melted away, however, as the idea that the principle of subsidiarity would be written into the legislation to regulate relations between different levels of government in Scotland had been dropped. Government lawyers were reported to have advised that the introduction of the principle into British law was anathema as it was apparently unjusticiable.

Sensitivity was also shown to concerns and anxieties of local government in Scotland, and to other unelected governmental bodies. They received attention in their own chapter of the White Paper but the reserved powers structure meant that it contained largely statements of the Government's intentions, with no substantive guarantees for the protection of Councils or Quangos. A body to look into the relationships between local government &

the Scottish Parliament was announced, however, which became the McIntosh Commission.

The entire White Paper was written in a much-praised, crisp, astringent style, but the subtleties contained within its elegance were nowhere better hidden than in the chapter on finance. Objectives, an assessment of the current arrangements and details of the new 'assigned budget' were all impeccably laid down. The operation of the Convention's agreed three-pence-in-the-pound income tax varying scheme was detailed and fleshed out from the Convention's model. Considerable attention was paid to local government expenditure and taxation. The subtlety was contained in the clarity of the statement of policy masking the delicate removal of all the Convention's commitments to placing the financial settlement firmly within the legislation. Further evidence of the mild retreat was present here too. Any recalibration of the Barnett formula was to be done after 'full consultation' rather than reaching 'mutual agreement'. Westminster's superiority was not to be challenged.

The electoral system agreed by the Convention made it intact into the White Paper - with the exception of the guarantee of 129 members mentioned above. The electoral agreement between Labour and the Liberal Democrats to ensure equal numbers of men and women in winnable candidacies at the first election had, however, not been translated into legislative proposal. The parties had been given a variety of advice about the legality of the agreement under UK and European equal opportunities law, and the Liberal Democrats had asked the Labour Government to include an exemption to existing law in the Scotland Bill scheme, to remove any chance of a legal challenge to their selection procedures. The White Paper urged the parties to do their best, but contained no exemption. Similarly, the Convention had agreed to outlaw 'dual mandates' (an MSP also being an MP, an MEP or a Councillor). 'Scotland's Parliament' left it to the individual political parties.

In almost every area the White Paper outlined a Scottish Parliament that would be much more powerful than the Assembly to have been created in 1978, with far more extensive powers, including fiscal powers. The White Paper offered an international and especially European role undreamed of in 1978. But differences between the electoral systems was the single issue which was to impinge most on the politics of 1997. The replacement of the crude 'double first-past-the-post' system contained in the 1978 Act with the relative sophistication of the Additional Member System (AMS) agreed by the Convention, would do more than simply create the first system of proportional representation for the British mainland. It would prevent the probability of domination of the new Parliament by one party and one region of Scotland. Great play was to be made of this argument in the referendum in areas outside the central belt.

The last chapters of the White Paper contained material that the Convention had not touched upon. The building that was to house the Parliament featured largely, prefacing Donald Dewar's controversial decision to site it in Holyrood and not Calton Hill. Extensive sections on staffing reflected, perhaps, civil service concerns, with eight paragraphs devoted to the subject, in comparison with only one on running costs. Outline details of Labour's two question referendum were given, this having been promised in 1996 when its unilateral announcement had put the Convention under very considerable strain. The briefest timetable for the Scotland Bill and the establishment of Scotland's new Parliament by the arrival of the millennium conclude the text.

With the White Paper published, the stage was set for the Referendum. A Yes-Yes campaign, Scotland Forward, had been in preparation since the Autumn of 1996 and on the strength of their view that nothing in the White Paper was an insuperable hurdle to independence, the SNP joined Labour and the Liberal Democrats for the duration. A No-No campaign, Think Twice, sprang to brief life. However, on September 11th 1997, Scotland's people voted quietly, determinedly and overwhelmingly for Scotland's Parliament.

Chapter Four:
The Scotland Bill and Act

Andy Myles

Published in December 1997, the Scotland Bill showed signs of further development from the White Paper. Where 'Scotland's Parliament' had the benefit of being written in political prose and allowed to express policy freely, the Bill had to be written in parliamentary language and consequently, there were major differences between the two.

Donald Dewar commented that the Bill was a truly historical document which was more a more radical piece of legislation than anyone could have imagined just six months previous. He stressed the similarity of the Bill to the White Paper, and added :

> 'It is not simply about Scotland. Nor is it in any sense routine reform, tinkering with the detail of our political system. It goes to the heart of our democracy, and offers hope for the democractic process itself'. (1)

The Bill proceeded through all stages in the Commons and the Lords, debated by the whole house and not in committee. Timetables had, however, been arranged between the parties, and the debates did not see any of the filibustering or harassment which had been such a feature in the late seventies. This was largely a consequence of the result of the referendum where the people of Scotland had voted 3 to 1 in favour of the Parliament and 2 to 1 for tax-varying powers. It also reflected the strange make-up of a House of Commons with no Conservatives from Scottish constituencies, and those from English constituencies grudgingly accepting the principle of the Bill. Debates were, therefore, more often between the supporters of home rule rather than with its opponents. The Bill was finalised in November 1998 in the House of Lords, receiving Royal Assent that month.

Part I, Section 1 begins with the simple and ringing clause 'There shall be a Scottish Parliament', and plunges straight into details of the electoral system. The Act lays down all of the mechanisms for Scottish Parliamentary General Elections using the Convention's Additional Member System (AMS), embellished only slightly by provisions to allow independents to stand in the list sections, and for the registration of political parties, (interlocking with Labour's proposals for this measure in a separate Act). Schedule 1 is brought into effect by Section 1 and contains the Government's belief that Scottish and Westminster constituencies must share boundaries. Arrangements for the filling of vacancies are detailed, as is the use of the local government franchise. The term of office of members is defined along with the grounds for disqualification and its effect.

Section 19 sees the introduction of the Presiding Officer and 'his' duties and deputies. It is worthy of note that while the general tenor of most of the Act is in tune with the Convention and White Paper proposals, and that the legislation is generally permissive, allowing the new Parliament to develop its own style of operation, in the matter of titles the Act is highly prescriptive. Thus we have 'Presiding Officer', 'Scottish Executive' and 'First Minister'. Where the Convention had agreed to disagree on the matter of titles, it will be interesting to see if the titles imposed by the Act survive. In the debates it was argued that it was essential that they are not confused with the Westminster terminology - and countered that this was a disingenuous ruse to assert the supremacy of London. It remains a mildly dissonant element of the Act.

The Presiding Officer's role as described in the Act is a highly significant, and largely logical, development of the earlier plans. The powers over the Parliament's proceedings, the Scottish Parliamentary Corporate Body (detailed in Schedule 2) and the guardianship of vires - the legislative competence and non-competence of the Scottish Parliament - all add to the role foreseen by the Convention.

The Act is largely permissive in respect of the proceedings of the new Parliament. Standing Orders are established in Section 22 but their content is minimal within the Act and within Schedule 3 which makes further provision. The Act does, on the other hand, contain significant provision for powers to call witnesses and documents. It also establishes immunity and protections for proceedings, including in respect of defamation, contempt of court and corrupt practices.

The power of the Parliament to legislate is established in Section 28 and subsequent sections lay down the scope of legislative competence. Schedule 4 details the Westminster Acts protected from modification. The Act creates a thicket of provisions around the Parliament to ensure that its Acts are intra vires (meaning within the legislative competence of the Scottish Parliament), including powers for the Presiding Officer, Scottish Ministers, the Secretary of State, the Law Officers and the Judicial Committee of the Privy Council.

In a further assertion of the supremacy of Westminster, the Act includes the brutally blunt 28 (7) 'This section does not affect the power of the Parliament of the United Kingdom to make laws for Scotland'. This is one of the few points where the Act blatantly contradicts 'Scotland's Parliament, Scotland's Right' and the Claim of Right upon which the Convention process was based. It demonstrates the sensitivity of Westminster to its claim of the sovereignty of the Crown in Parliament. In a further embellishment of the Convention scheme, Acts of the new Parliament are to require Royal Assent under Section 32.

Schedule 5 of the Act lists the powers reserved to the Westminster Parliament. It contained few surprises when it was published, largely comprised of detailed lists of the constitutional, macro-economic, social security, foreign affairs immigration and nationality and business regulation matters always destined to remain at Westminster. The Schedule does contain, however, some bones of contention. Further to the indications contained in the White Paper, abortion and other issues where criminal law, medicine and morality meet, are reserved, where the Convention had assumed that these powers would be devolved. Limited powers over broadcasting, equal opportunities and monopolies and mergers that the Convention saw as being devolved are, similarly, on the reserved list in the Act. It will be of interest to see if these reserved powers remain, and possibly an early test of the flexibility of arrangements for the transfer of powers.

Part II of the Act establishes the Scottish Administration. Sections 44 to 50 create the 'First Minister', ministers, junior ministers and the Scottish law officers. Again, the Queen plays an unanticipated part in the appointment of ministers, but the politics of appointment is largely in line with the Convention scheme and the Act is permissive rather than prescriptive with regard to the structure of the 'Scottish Executive'. Section 51, meanwhile, cements the civil service into the Home Civil Service. The development of a Scottish civil service over the last century as a major element in Scottish civic life has been much commented upon. The further development of the civil service under the Scottish Parliament and Executive will be instructive (see Chapter Eight).

Section 52 allows for the exercise of statutory functions by Scottish ministers, and Section 53 provides for the transfer of the powers of the current Scottish Office to them. Section 54 limits the exercise of ministerial functions to the devolved areas and Section 55 and 56 prepare for areas where Westminster and Holyrood ministers will be required to share powers or operate them in agreement.

The relationship of the new Parliament and the European Union featured large in the White Paper, but in the Act much less is said. Section 29 debars law-making by the Parliament, and Section 57 debars administrative action and secondary legislation by the Executive, if contrary to EU Directives. No legislative form is given to the White Paper pledge that the new institutions will be thoroughly involved in European decision making. During the Westminster debates the Government rejected all amendments designed to secure rights for the Scottish Executive in European Affairs. Scottish participation is to be at the invitation only of Westminster, identified as a potential flashpoint of the new constitutional arrangements during Westminster debates on the Bill.

Part III of the Act covers financial provisions and here we meet the second major missing item. Section 64(2) states that 'the Secretary of State shall from time to time make payments into the Scottish Consolidated Fund out of money provided by Parliament of such amounts as he may determine'.There is no reference to a formula, or the principles of equalisation so forthrightly annunciated by the Convention, and no 'full consultation' let alone mutual agreement with regard to the future of the Barnett Formula (see Chapter Nine). In the Act, the 'block' is left naked. The financial sections are largely technical, covering payments from the Scottish Consolidated Fund, strictly limited borrowing and lending, audit, financial control and accounts. These technical aspects are again, fairly limited and rather permissive. The new institutions are to be trusted insofar as accounting is concerned. But as far as the politics of Scottish finance are concerned the Treasury in Whitehall has the whip hand. The New Labour Government has offered the commitments given in the White Paper, but no law binds the decisions of future Governments. This was, again, identified as a potential flashpoint for dispute in the future.

Part IV of the Act provides for the tax varying power as agreed in the Convention with the technicalities required to bring it into effect. The Act guarantees also that the value of the three-pence-in-the-pound income tax will be sustained as a proportion against both inflation and changes in the system of taxation. Scottish taxpayers are defined and accounting procedures provided. The effect of tax reduction is defined and the Treasury given supplemental powers to enable the tax varying mechanism to operate.

Part V covers miscellaneous and general provisions including remuneration of MSPs (Sections 81-83), the oath of allegiance (84) and exemption from jury service (85), all of which added to the Convention and White Paper provisions. Scottish representation at Westminster is dealt with in Section 86. The Convention had agreed that this was a matter for Westminster, after Labour had urged that the numbers of Scottish MPs remain protected. The change from this position was now completed and the Act allowed for the reduction at the next Westminster boundary review to numbers justified by Scotland's population. The knock-on effect will be the reduced number of MSPs because of the decision upon shared boundaries. This is another issue best watched, as it quite probably means MSPs competing with each other for significantly reduced numbers of seats for the election in May 2007, and a degree of internal instability in all Scotland's political parties in the period up to then.

Cross-border bodies are provided for in Sections 88-90. These are to be listed by Order in Council but broadly cover public bodies operating in fields only partially reserved. The sections put in place powers to modify the operation of the bodies as the home rule settlement evolves. Maladministration is dealt with in Section 91 followed by sections on the Queen's printer for Scotland, agency arrangements, private legislation, the appointment and removal of judges, and so forth, with a variety of provisions additional to those outlined in the White Paper, but no doubt essential to the proper functioning of Scottish democracy.

Part VI deals with supplementary matters and particularly provides for the making of subordinate legislation, details of the various procedures for which comprise Schedule 7. It also makes effective Schedule 8 which amends a whole raft of Westminster Acts, modifying them to fit the Scotland Act. Schedule 9 contains repeals of sections of a number of Westminster Acts for the same purpose.

The Scotland Act 1998 sets out a Parliament much more powerful than that of the Scotland Act 1978. This is perhaps best symbolised in the very use of the word 'Parliament' as opposed to 'Assembly'. In the seventies the Scotland Act was a slightly panicky response to the rise of political nationalism. The Scotland Act 1998 is to a far greater extent the reflection of the 'settled will of the Scottish people'.

Chapter Five:
The Powers of the Parliament

Andrew Burns

The Shape of **Things to Come**

The main recommendations of the Scotland Act 1998 can be summarised as:

- the Parliament should be elected by some other method than first-past-the-post. The method finally agreed was the Additional Member System (AMS).

- its working structures and patterns should enable equal representation of ethnic and other groups, and ensure the transparency of its work.

- the Parliament's powers are to cover all functions of government currently devolved to the Scottish Office.

- the Parliament should sanction an office for Scottish representation in Brussels.

- a single tier of local government.

- the Islands area requires special constitutional status.

- a Charter of Rights should guarantee fundamental rights within Scottish law.

The Scotland Act, as above, finally received Royal Assent in November 1998. It differs in one fundamental way to the most recent and ill-fated Scotland Act 1978. The 1978 Act listed all powers to be devolved to Scotland, those not, were reserved to Westminster. The 1998 Act does the reverse as the powers to be reserved to the Westminster Parliament are listed and everything else is devolved.

Clearly the new model is more powerful from a devolutionary standpoint. Where there is doubt, the onus is on the matter being a devolved issue under the competence of the Scottish Parliament.

It is not possible to go into the exact details of the 1998 Act (it is over 40,000 words long, with 116 clauses), but very broadly, the Act indicates that Westminster will retain powers and responsibilities for five main areas :

- defence
- foreign affairs
- central economic policies (including business taxation)
- social security
- immigration.

The Scottish Parliament will have competence over all other areas, taking over powers and responsibilities of the existing Scottish Office. This will give democratic control and accountability over Scottish internal affairs, including health, education and training, local government, social work and housing, economic development and transport, law and home affairs, environment, agriculture, forestry and fishing, sport and the arts, and other related matters.

These ten main headings are outlined in more detail below. Even the most cursory reading indicates that the forthcoming Scottish Parliament will have competence over almost every area of domestic legislation affecting the ordinary Scottish voter.

Health:

- health, including overall responsibility for the National Health Service in Scotland, the education and training of health professionals, and terms and conditions for NHS staff and general practitioners.

Education and Training:

- school education, including pre-5, primary and secondary education, Her Majesty's Inspectorate of Schools, and the supply, training and terms and conditions of teachers.
- further and higher education, including policy, funding, the functions of the Scottish Higher Education Funding Council (SHEFC) and student support.
- science and research funding, except the UK Research Councils.
- training policy and lifelong learning including all the existing training responsibilities of the Scottish Office.

- vocational qualifications including the Scottish Qualifications Authority.
- careers advice and guidance.

Local Government:

- local government, including local government finance and domestic and non-domestic taxation.

Social Work and Housing:

- social work, including the Children's Hearings system.
- voluntary sector issues.
- housing, including Scottish Homes.
- area regeneration, including the designation of enterprise zones.
- land-use planning, and building control.

Economic Development and Transport:

- economic development including Scottish Enterprise, Highlands and Islands Enterprise, and local enterprise companies.
- financial assistance to industry, subject to common UK guidelines and consultation arrangements to be published later.
- inward investment, including the functions of Locate in Scotland.
- promotion of trade and exports, including Scottish Trade International.
- promotion of tourism, including the Scottish Tourist Board.
- passenger and road transport, including the Scottish road network, road safety, bus policy, concessionary fares, cycling, taxis and minicabs, non-technical aspects of disability and transport, some rail grant powers, the Strathclyde Passenger Transport Executive, and consultation arrangements in respect of public transport.
- appropriate air and sea transport powers covering ports, harbours and piers, freight shipping and ferry services, Highlands and Islands Airports Ltd, and other planning and environmental issues relating to airports.
- inland waterways.

Law and Home Affairs

- criminal law and procedure, except for offences created in statute law relating to reserved matters including drugs and firearms.

- civil law.

- electoral law, in relation to local government elections.

- judicial appointments, subject to the appointments of the Lord President of the Court of Session and the Lord Justice Clerk made by The Queen, advised by the Prime Minister, on nomination from the Scottish Executive.

- the criminal justice and prosecution system.

- the civil and criminal courts.

- tribunals concerned with devolved matters.

- legal aid.

- parole, the release of life prisoners and alleged miscarriages of justice.

- prisons, including the Scottish Prison Service and treatment of offenders.

- the police and fire services including fire safety.

- civil defence and emergency planning.

- functions under various international legal agreements in devolved areas, for example relating to child abduction and the reciprocal enforcement of Maintenance Orders.

- liquor licensing.

- protecting animals including domestic, captive and wild animals, zoo licensing, dangerous wild animals and game, also control of dogs, boarding kennels and dangerous dogs.

Environment:

- the environment, including environmental protection, air, land and water pollution, the Scottish Environment Protection Agency, water supplies and sewerage, and policies to promote sustainable development within the international commitments agreed by the UK.

- the natural heritage including countryside issues and the functions of Scottish Natural Heritage.

- the built heritage including the functions of Historic Scotland.
- flood prevention, coast protection and reservoir safety.

Agriculture, Forestry and Fishing:

- agriculture including responsibility for implementing measures under the Common Agricultural Policy, and for domestic agriculture including crofting, animal and plant health and animal welfare.
- food standards.
- forestry - the Secretary of State for Scotland's functions including power of direction over the Forestry Commission, will be transferred to the Scottish Executive, as will responsibility for finance for Forestry Commission activities in Scotland.
- fisheries including responsibility for implementing measures under the Common Fisheries Policy, subject to suitable co-ordination arrangements to ensure effective discharge of UK obligations, domestic fisheries matters including inshore fisheries, salmon and freshwater fisheries and aquaculture.

Sport and The Arts:

- sport, including the Scottish Sports Council.
- the arts, including the National Library of Scotland, the National Museums of Scotland, the National Galleries of Scotland, the Scottish Museums Council, the Scottish Arts Council, Scottish Screen and support for Gaelic.

Other Matters:

- statistics, public registers and records, including responsibilities of the Keeper of the Registers, the Keeper of the Records, and the Registrar General for Scotland.

From the brief discussion above, it is clear that the Constitutional Convention 'vision' now broadly on the statute book through the 1998 Scotland Act was firmly based on the belief that Scotland (and the whole of the United Kingdom) needed to enter a new political era. Scotland was seen as potentially playing a pioneering role in modernising the United Kingdom constitution and challenging out-dated assumptions that have constrained democracy in the UK.

The devolutionary proposals outlined indicate that the old political divides, which remain stubbornly in place at Westminster, face unalterable change within Scotland. Scotland has had a unique and enviable opportunity to devise a new Parliament fit for the 21st century, and it appears that this opportunity has not been squandered. The new system of government in Scotland will be built on lasting principles which will enhance democracy, and help restore faith in the political process.

The really hard work starts now though. Despite the best efforts of all concerned to construct this new system, it will be the operational aspects of the Scottish Parliament that will be crucial to its longevity and perceived success. The best foundations have been laid, and it is clear that the Parliament will have a huge policy capacity. Envisioning that policy capacity has been one thing, the politicians elected on May 6th 1999 will soon have to start its implementation. It is clear that they will have plenty of scope to either succeed or fail.

Chapter Six:
How the Parliament will Work

Andrew Burns

As discussed in the previous chapter, the White Paper 'Scotland's Parliament' set out the Government's detailed proposals, drawing on the Scottish Constitutional Convention's recommendations on the composition and powers of the Scottish Parliament. It stated however that the Government wished as far as possible to leave detailed decisions about how the Parliament should work to the Parliament itself. It was expected:

> 'That the Scottish Parliament will adopt modern methods of working; that it will be accessible, open and responsive to the needs of the public; that participation by organisations and individuals in decision-making will be encouraged; and that views and advice from specialists will be sought as appropriate'. (1)

The Government's aim was that the Parliament:

> 'Once in being, should have the necessary room to evolve in its own way, rather than be forced along a rigid pre-determined path'. (2)

This was accepted by the Secretary of State for Scotland who announced on November 14th 1997 his intention to establish an all-Party Consultative Steering Group (CSG), to consider how the Parliament might operate. It will be up to Members of the Scottish Parliament (MSPs) to accept them. The Scottish Office Minister for Home Affairs and Devolution, Henry McLeish MP, chaired the Group and stated that the Scottish Parliament should decide how it operates. However, it would clearly be unreasonable to expect MSPs to draw up Standing Orders and develop operating rules for the Parliament, immediately after the first elections.

The CSG was charged to report to Donald Dewar by the end of 1998, and published its final report just beyond schedule in January 1999. Draft Standing Orders will now be prepared on the basis of the report, to be presented to the Parliament. The Group's remit was wide, as Donald Dewar stated, at the formal announcement of the launching of the CSG :

'The task facing this group should not be underestimated. Developing a new politics for a new millennium is a significant challenge in anyone's book. The group starts with a blank sheet of paper and hopefully a lot of ideas. The Group is drafting ideas from scratch. Among the key issues to be considered are how should the Parliament conduct its day to day business? How will the Parliament turn ideas and policies into laws? What should the Parliament make of pre-legislative committees? How can modern technology best be used to make the Parliament open, accessible and efficient?' (3)

The CSG was asked to agree to a number of broad principles that should be followed in preparing for the Scottish Parliament, and to consider any specific proposals which might emerge. The group was supported by Scottish Office officials, able to draw on advice from various experts in taking forward detailed work for further consideration. These included relevant constitutional and other experts who could advise on the procedures for the Parliament.

The Scotland Act requires the proceedings of the Scottish Parliament to be regulated by Standing Orders (Clause 22). Schedule 3 makes further provision as regards the contents of the Standing Orders, and various other provisions in the Act specify matters, which must be covered by Standing Orders.

The provisions in the Scotland Act set out the 'minimum requirement', which must be covered in the Standing Orders. These provide a basic framework, which can be built upon and are listed below:

'Minimum Requirements' from the Scotland Act:

- Elections of the Presiding Officer (PO) and the First Minister
- Preservation of Order
- Proceedings to be in public except in such circumstances as Standing Orders provide
- Reporting and publishing proceedings
- The appointment of members to Committees
- Crown Interests/Queen's Consent
- Registration and declaration of members' interests
- Exercise of the PO's functions

- Participation of PO and his deputies in parliamentary proceedings
- Appointment of members to the Scottish Parliamentary Corporate Body
- Summoning of witnesses and documents by committees
- Participation in Parliamentary procedures by Lord Advocate or Solicitor General
- Scrutiny of Bills by PO
- Submission of Bills for Royal Assent by PO
- Stages of Bills
- Financial controls, accounts and audit
- Procedures for Tax-varying resolutions
- Arrangements for the swearing in of MSPs and Ministers
- Matters relating to constituency and regional vacancies

The Standing Orders can, and in some cases will, inevitably go further than minimum requirements set out in the Bill. Matters such as the working hours of the Parliament, number of sitting days, the procedures for the taking of the oath and for the elections of the Presiding Officer and the First Minister need to be decided. Consideration will need to be given to the number and remits of committees and the split between plenary and committee work.

All the main political parties have agreed to participate in the Consultative Steering Group. Their agreement to come together to contribute to the development of ideas at such an early stage bodes well for the future of the Parliament and the political process based on consensus in Scotland.

The Group met for the first time on January 19th 1998, and agreed a three-point draft remit:

- To bring together views on and consider the operational needs and working methods of the Scottish Parliament.
- To develop proposals for the rules and procedures and Standing Orders, which the Parliament may be invited to adopt.
- To prepare a report to the Secretary of State for Scotland by the end of 1998, to inform the preparation of draft Standing Orders. (4)

This remit does not prevent the Scottish Parliament from amending its own Standing Orders but it is likely that the inaugural 1999 Standing Orders will be those recommended by the CSG to the Secretary of State for Scotland. All the above quite clearly indicates that Scotland's new politics will be radically different from that currently practised at Westminster.

It would appear five sets of guiding principles underpin this so-called 'New Politics':

Accountability

The structures of the Scottish Parliament will ensure its accountability to the electorate.

Openness and access

The Scottish Parliament will develop clear and open objectives through a transparent policy-making process. Greater openness of proceedings will encourage public and civic bodies to play a more dynamic role by encouraging participation at all stages of the legislative process.

Distribution of power

The Scottish Parliament will include a series of checks and balances so that the Executive does not exercise disproportionate power, as in Westminster. The House of Commons is the primary check on the excesses of the Executive but it is failing in this role. A strong committee structure will allow the Scottish Parliament to do its job properly. The Committees will be powerful and proportionate to party strength in composition. They will also be able to initiate and scrutinise legislation and to conduct inquiries into administrative matters of public concern.

Representativeness and participation

Members of the Scottish Parliament should reflect the diversity of Scotland's population and give voice to Scotland-wide interests. Standing Orders will provide for imaginative ways to increase participation.

Consensus and co-operation

It is important that the Scottish Parliament should have an effective decision-making process, but not to the exclusion of co-operation, deliberation, and consensus. MSPs should put aside their sectional and adversarial interests and work together for the common good of Scotland. It is accepted that it is now time to build on the foundations laid by the Scottish Constitutional Convention, which were consolidated by the Scotland Act.

The Convention further argued that systems of Government should not create Executive dominance over a Parliament. The Westminster Parliament is often incapable of guaranteeing thorough scrutiny of legislation. Parliamentary Committees should have a greater role than the Westminster model in ensuring accountability from the Executive and scrutinising legislation.

The system of permanent Scottish Parliamentary Committees will have a formal role in the legislative process, with the power to hold the Executive to account. The Committees will therefore build a constructive relationship with Ministers in preparing and scrutinising legislation.

To do this, the CSG has recommended that Committees should be able to take advice from experts and interested parties. This would encourage more thoughtful consideration of legislation, and eliminate potential problems in the drafting, purpose and implementation of a Bill. A more thoughtful and considered approach would promote better scrutiny of legislation and create more opportunities for the constructive amendment of legislation. In addition, allowing Committees to initiate legislation would increase their stature enormously. The power to initiate legislation would create a committee system with an integral role in the legislative process and act as a powerful constraint on the Executive. Westminster with its antiquated procedures and practices is clearly failing to scrutinise government activity, or to hold government to account.

But just what are these 'Standing Orders' recommended by the CSG? Standing Orders are rules that regulate proceedings. (5) Standing Orders are commonplace, governing not only the House of Commons but also local government, schools, and civic organisations up and down the country.

Standing Orders sound boring, dusty and irrelevant to the democratic agenda, but are at the heart of any democracy. The operational aspects of the Scottish Parliament will be crucial to its future effectiveness, and all citizens must have a say in how the Parliament regulates itself. The CSG was set up to examine and recommend a set of Standing Orders to the Secretary of State, and this is a welcome step towards an inclusive and consensual process.

The present Westminster model of Standing Orders is the product of centuries of constitutional and political development in the UK. This process has been characterised by evolutionary democratic development, and consequently a parliamentary system based on custom and tradition has been produced.

This is a unique opportunity for Scotland to devise procedures more suited to its own civic tradition and the 21st century. Donald Dewar MP, Secretary of State for Scotland, has highlighted this very point. Talking recently about the Scottish Parliament he said:

> *'It will be free to develop procedures and working practices which are in tune with the norms of the 1990's not the 19th century'.(6)*

The importance of Standing Orders is clearly emphasised by Crick and Millar in 'To Make the Parliament of Scotland a Model for Democracy':

> *'A new and national Parliament has an opportunity to innovate, not merely to create and adopt procedures more effective and responsive to public opinion than those of Westminster, but to show Westminster and other centres of power that new ways are needed, can work and are better'. (7)*

Crick and Millar highlight the importance of the CSG's work:

> *'Scotland's Parliament will only work, as its supporters want it to work, for and with the Scottish people, if from the word go it is bold enough to break from the Westminster mould and to invent and adapt procedures and working practices better-suited to and arising from Scotland's more democratic civic traditions'. (9)*

But why be different from Westminster? The answer lies not just in Scotland's democratic civic traditions but in the plain fact that Westminster does not work. The traditional Government-Opposition confrontational nature, with excessive parliamentary control held through the Whips Office, is commonly criticised. These structures impact directly on the quality of legislation coming from the House of Commons.

Senior Government members in Scotland also hold these concerns.

Donald Dewar MP, in a speech to the 'Charter88/Economist' Constitutional Convention on July 11th 1997, stated that:

> 'Devolution has the scope to modernise the processes of politics. A Scottish Parliament will be elected on a more proportional basis. It is unlikely that any one party will dominate - and so there will need to be much more emphasis on consensus building'. (9)

Henry McLeish MP, Scottish Office Minister for Home Affairs and Devolution, speaking at the Bavarian State Chancellery during a visit to discuss devolution in October 1997 said:

> 'My meeting today has reinforced my strong belief that a Scottish Parliament will serve Scotland's needs far better if it replaces the confrontational style of politics of Westminster with a new approach based on consensus and co-operation'. (10)

Systems of government should not include Executive dominance over Parliament as has evolved in Westminster. The Westminster Parliament is often incapable of guaranteeing thorough scrutiny of legislation. Scottish Parliament Committees should have a greater role than their Westminster counterparts in ensuring accountability from the Executive and scrutinising legislation.

A Scottish Parliament with a more representative legislature, an accountable civil service, a more open governing culture, and enforceable rights, will mean Scots becoming embryonic citizens in a culture of popular sovereignty. These five guiding principles, as discussed above, form the basis of the modernisation of politics in Scotland:

- accountability
- openness and access
- distribution of power
- representativeness and participation
- consensus and co-operation

These are set to have a symbiotic relationship with the rest of the United Kingdom body-politic. They have grown outside the UK system and moved away from the Westminster model, yet in their development as a new kind of politics and practice for the UK, they may now in turn, demand a response from the political system at its centre.

Chapter Seven: The Scottish Executive

Noreen Burrows

The Scottish Executive is the term used in the Scotland Act to describe what is, effectively, the Scottish government for all devolved matters. Before the elections take place it is impossible to predict what exactly the Scottish Executive will look like but it is possible to describe some of the posts, which need to be filled. There will be:

- A First Minister

- Ministers and Junior Ministers appointed by the First Minister

- The Lord Advocate and the Solicitor General for Scotland.

Together these will be known as the Scottish Ministers. No one can be a Scottish Minister and a Minister of the Crown in the UK government. So, for example, the same person could not be the Secretary of State for Scotland (a member of the UK government) and First Minister in the Scottish Executive.

Appointments to Ministerial Posts

The First Minister

After the elections take place in May, one of the first tasks of the Parliament will be to select its First Minister. Any MSP can be proposed, but the person chosen must enjoy sufficient support in Parliament to be able to lead the Scottish Executive and get government business through. Nominations will be submitted to the Presiding Officer and, if there is more than one nomination, an election will be held. The Consultative Steering Group (CSG) suggests that a series of elections might be needed until the name of one candidate emerges.

If one party secures a majority of seats then the leader of that party in the Parliament will be elected. In all likelihood either Donald Dewar or Alex Salmond will be elected, given the strengths of the Labour Party and the SNP in opinion polls. Once the Parliament has elected a candidate, the Presiding Officer will recommend them to the Queen, who will make the appointment.

Thereafter a new First Minister must be elected:

- after a general election
- if the existing First Minister resigns, for example after a vote of no confidence
- if the office becomes vacant, for example if the First Minister dies in office or if he/she becomes a Minister of the Crown in the UK government (either by being given a peerage or by being simultaneously an MP)
- if the First Minister ceases to be an MSP

Scottish Ministers

The First Minister will choose other Scottish Ministers from amongst the MSPs. Before they can be appointed to their posts, Parliament must approve the First Minister's selection of ministers. The CSG recommends that Parliament should be able to approve ministers individually or en bloc by a simple majority vote. Parliament could not, however, substitute individuals as the power to nominate lies with the First Minister. The First Minister cannot choose Scottish Ministers from outside the ranks of the Scottish Parliament, for example, from the House of Commons or House of Lords.

The First Minister will decide how many ministers he/she wishes to appoint and what responsibilities each will have. The Labour Party seems to favour a fairly small ministerial team, as compared to the SNP, which would prefer a much larger one. How many ministers are needed and the extent of their responsibilities will depend on the priorities of the political parties but ministers are likely to be needed for housing, education, health, economic development, environment, agriculture and transport. A minister with financial responsibilities may be needed or a Minister for Europe or External affairs. Any or all of these portfolios might be shared. The First Minister can dismiss any Scottish Minister or reshuffle his/her cabinet team as need arises.

The First Minister can look beyond his/her own party to appoint ministers. Again this will depend on the outcome of the elections and how MSPs choose to operate. In the event of a coalition, some ministerial posts might be shared amongst the coalition partners, as is the case in Germany where the Social Democratic Party shares cabinet posts with the Green Party.

Junior Scottish Ministers

The First Minister may also appoint Junior Ministers to assist Scottish Ministers. They would be selected and hold office under the same terms as Scottish Ministers.

The Lord Advocate and the Solicitor General for Scotland

Unlike other members of the Scottish Executive, the Lord Advocate and the Solicitor General need not be MSPs, because of their specialist role as government lawyers. There may not be any suitably qualified candidates amongst those elected to the Parliament. Both the Lord Advocate and the Solicitor General will be appointed by the Queen on the recommendation of the First Minister and after obtaining the approval of Parliament. The CSG is recommending that a simple majority vote is sufficient to demonstrate such approval. The Lord Advocate and the Solicitor General will be able to participate in the work of the Parliament, if they are not MSPs, for example by answering questions or taking part in debates or discussions in committees but they cannot vote.

The Secretary of State for Scotland

Despite the title of this post, the Secretary of State for Scotland is not a Scottish Minister. The Secretary of State for Scotland is an existing post within the UK government and will remain as such for the time being. The person holding this post is a member of the Westminster Parliament and a member of the UK Cabinet. In the longer term this might change, but at the moment this is not clear. MPs from Scottish constituencies in the Westminster Parliament and Scottish peers will still be eligible to hold ministerial posts in the UK government, and are accountable to the Westminster Parliament.

The Functions of the Scottish Executive

The Scottish Executive will have a number of powers and responsibilities. Some are outlined in the Scotland Act, with others still to be defined. The most important tasks facing the Scottish Executive are :

* to carry out statutory functions laid down in the Scotland Act

* to carry out functions transferred to them from Ministers of the Crown, under rules applying before the Scotland Act came into force

- to share powers with Ministers of the Crown where devolved and reserved matters overlap e.g. in relation to European matters.

Functions laid down in the Scotland Act

The most important task of the Scottish Executive is in policy development and delivery in all devolved matters. It is expected that Scottish Ministers will propose the main legislative business of the Parliament shortly after an election. The CSG suggest that the Executive should announce fairly detailed plans for the forthcoming year and outline plans for the rest of the parliamentary session. These should set out policies which the Scottish Executive wishes to pursue and how it intends to achieve its policy goals. It will be the task of the relevant Scottish Minister to steer legislation through the processes described in Chapter Six. In particular he/she will play an active role in consulting and discussing the contents of a Bill and its financial, administrative and legal implications. The Scottish Minister responsible for the Bill will be required to state that its subject matter is within the devolved powers of the Parliament. This assessment must take into account limitations imposed by the Scotland Act and that legislation, if enacted, will not breach any rule of European Union (EU) law or any right protected by the European Convention on Human Rights.

Scottish Ministers must also provide detailed estimates of how they wish to spend monies made available from the block grant. If they wish Parliament to use the tax varying powers they must initiate a motion to Parliament explaining their rationale. Scottish Ministers must arrange to publish and present their accounts to Parliament.

Functions transferred from Ministers of the Crown to Scottish Ministers

Most powers currently exercised by ministers in the Scottish Office will, after the elections, be transferred to the Scottish Ministers. There is a mass of existing legislation, for example on housing, health, education, which enables ministers to carry out policies by issuing circulars or instructions which set out what has to be done to implement a policy. Ministers can also make subordinate or delegated legislation setting out the detailed rules for the application of a 'parent act'. These powers, with some exceptions, are transferred to the Scottish Ministers. Detailed rules on how Parliament will approve delegated legislation are to be adopted.

Sharing powers with Ministers of the Crown

Some powers that are transferred to the Scottish Ministers will be shared with Ministers of the Crown and practices will have to be developed to decide which Minister should take a particular action. For example, how a directive issued by the EU will be implemented. Implementation of directives is a shared power so both the Scottish Minister and the Minister of the Crown will be able to introduce delegated legislation implementing directives in Scotland. Some accommodation will need to be reached to determine the best course of action in these circumstances. (For more information on European matters see Chapter Fifteen).

Co-ordination between the Scottish Ministers and the UK government will be vital in many areas to ensure that policy is co-ordinated north and south of the border. Two ideas are currently under discussion to find the right kind of framework in which such co-ordination can take place:

- by way of concordats
- in a joint ministerial committee.

Concordats

A concordat is a non-statutory agreement between the Scottish Executive and the UK. These are currently being developed although cannot be agreed until the Scottish Executive comes into being. Two types of concordats are being proposed. Overarching concordats will lay down procedures to be followed by all departments on matters such as European affairs or statistical information. Bilateral concordats will set out the arrangements between a government department in the UK and its Scottish equivalent, for example on health or agriculture. Concordats will be reviewed and monitored regularly to ensure that liaison is effective.

Joint Ministerial Committee

Once the devolved administrations begin, it is proposed that a Joint Ministerial Committee is established with representatives of the UK government and all the devolved administrations to discuss policy matters of communal interest. The Committee would be advisory only and its decisions would not bind any party. It will be particularly important to discuss issues where overlap between devolved and reserved responsibilities exists. Again it must be repeated that until the devolved executives are up and running these arrangements cannot be agreed and may be rejected or replaced by other forms of liaison. However, whatever the political complexion of any part of the UK, it is clear that some kind of talking shop must exist to reach a view on a wide variety of policies that affect the UK as a whole. (See also Chapter Eighteen).

Relationship between Executive and Parliament

In any system of parliamentary democracy, the main function of a Parliament is to hold the government to account. Accountability is therefore at the heart of the relationship between the Scottish Executive and the Scottish Parliament, and this is summed up in two of the principles adopted by the CSG:

- the Scottish Parliament should embody and reflect the sharing of power between the people of Scotland, the legislators and the Scottish Executive.

- the Scottish Executive should be accountable to the Scottish Parliament and the Parliament and the Executive should be accountable to the people of Scotland.

A key task of the Parliament will be to examine how the Scottish Executive is governing Scotland - are its policies meaningful, do they serve Scotland's needs, do they work, is public money being spent wisely and are government departments value for money? To allow MSPs to do this, the Scottish Executive will need to provide information to the Parliament and be prepared to answer questions to individual MSPs. The Scottish Parliament will be small enough to allow its members to get to know both one another and members of the Scottish Executive and it is likely in these circumstances that information will flow more readily. One of the problems that dogs Westminster is the culture of secrecy and it has been one of the aims of the Scottish Constitutional Convention and the CSG to ensure that a culture of openness and accessibility prevails in Scotland.

The formal means by which MSPs will scrutinise the work of the Executive will be laid down in Standing Orders once the Parliament is up and running. The CSG is recommending that these Standing Orders should cover the following:

- an annual debate in plenary on the Executive's legislative programme and budget, and an annual debate on its progress.

- general debates throughout the year on government policy.

- ministerial statements on specific issues of public policy, followed by a short debate.

- the use of votes of no confidence on the First Minister, the Scottish Executive or a named minister. A vote of no confidence in the First Minister or the entire Scottish Executive must lead to resignation although the rule does not apply where a named minister is subject to such a vote.

- committees of the Parliament will have the power to conduct enquiries and, in the course of these enquiries, to question ministers and civil servants and to take evidence.

- individuals ministers will appear before relevant subject committees to outline policy proposals and to discuss their work.

- special rules will be adopted on financial matters including the appointment of an Auditor General for Scotland, the creation of an audit committee and a debate on budgetary matters.

- Parliament will be able to appoint an Ombudsman to investigate complaints of maladministration against any member of the Scottish Executive.

Taken together with the rules requiring Parliament to approve the appointment of the Scottish Ministers, these procedures and mechanisms should allow Parliament to scrutinise the work of the Scottish Executive and hold it to account. Parliament has the ultimate sanction of a vote of no confidence that will trigger a resignation of either the entire Executive or the First Minister. No confidence votes will be rare if the Scottish Executive works effectively with the Parliament. A culture of openness and responsiveness in the day-to-day working of government is infinitely more effective than forcing a resignation after a policy has failed.

Chapter Eight:
The Scottish Civil Service

Richard Parry

Properly stated, the 'Scottish Civil Service' does not exist, before or after devolution. Section 51 of the Scotland Act makes it clear that service of the Scottish Administration (the official term) shall be service in the Home Civil Service. The White Paper does not make an explicit justification for this but suggests (para 10.12) that continuing interchange with other Government Departments 'will give the Scottish Executive the support of a tried and tested civil service machine, and access to a wide pool of talent and experience'.

In practice, this decision was much less significant than it was in the 1970s. Since 1996, recruitment, pay and gradings for all civil servants below the Senior Civil Service level have been devolved to departments. While the Executive will have to follow the basic structure of a non-partisan civil service recruited on merit on terms set out in the Civil Service Management Code, it will not have to seek Whitehall approval for its main organisational and personnel management decisions. For the around two hundred members of the Senior Civil Service in the Scottish Administration, the principle of a UK-wide service will apply, but decisions here on pay and promotions are individual ones and increasingly subject to outside advertisement. Perhaps more significant is that the Scottish Administration will continue to draw upon fast-stream recruitment procedures for its future heads.

Three further points stand out from Table Six. Most civil servants in Scotland are not in the Scottish Office at all but in a wide range of more labour-intensive functions that will not be devolved: the Ministry of Defence and the Department of Social Security have about 9,000 each. Even within the devolved administration most staff will be working in civil service executive agencies, with their own structure of accountable management under their Chief Executives, an autonomy they are expected to maintain. The Scottish Prison Service is the biggest entity in the devolved administration. And finally there are some Scottish civil servants not formally part of the Scottish Office (like those responsible to the Lord Advocate) which might now be integrated, most notably in a 'Ministry of Justice'.

Table Six: Full-time Equivalent Civil Servants in Scotland 1997-98

Total	46,160
In the devolved Scottish Administration	13,724
Scottish Office core	3,650
Agencies	
Scottish Prison Service	4,784
Scottish Courts Service	858
Historic Scotland	781
Scottish Fisheries Protection Agency	305
Fisheries Research Services	253
Scottish Office Pensions Agency	173
Student Awards Agency for Scotland	146
Scottish Agricultural Science Agency	127
Other Scottish departments	
Registers of Scotland	1,056
General Register Office for Scotland	219
Scottish Courts Administration	135
Scottish Record Office	131
Lord Advocate's Department, Crown Office and Procurator Fiscal Service	1,106

Sources: Departmental Reports 1998/99 of Departments of the Secretary of State for Scotland (Cm 3914, Appendix 5) and the Crown Office (Cm 3909 table 3); Digest of Scottish Statistics 1998 Table 6B5. (There are slight discrepancies of date and coverage between sources).

The shape of civil service life after devolution is particularly speculative. Unlike the way that choices on procedures in the Scottish Parliament have been made through the non-partisan Consultative Steering Group (CSG), decision-making is much less far advanced. Planning within the Scottish Office started around the turn of 1999 and 1999 at a strategic level and in the details of implementation, but final decisions on how the Scottish civil service will organise itself can only be taken by the political majority after the May elections. The low-profile practicality of many of the transitional questions needs to be emphasised - who the accounting officers will be (the senior civil servants answerable to Parliament for financial control), where ministers will be located, how suitable existing office accommodation will be, the corporate identity of the Administration and how the civil service will meet requirements of the Parliament.

The starting point for the post-devolution civil service is the Scottish Office as it has evolved. Its main long-term theme has been consolidation and integration from a basis of differentiation. The Scottish Office was a federation in 1939 of previously separate departments, and not until the 1970s were Central Services formed, to provide personnel and finance functions to departments. The Scottish Office, as an entity embracing constituent departments, dates only from the 1980s. The most recent reorganisation of 1995 departed from the old model in two ways - departments were made non-uniform and more like the directorates of Whitehall departments (eg Health and Home, previously seen as too small to be separate, were divided) and some functions were linked in an innovative way not found in Whitehall (environmental protection with agriculture, industry and urban policy with education).

Devolution threatens to reverse this 40-year process of corporate bonding. The new departments will be competitors for money, media attention and parliamentary time. There will be pressure to inflate their number to provide jobs for coalition partners, signal concern with issues and build up capability in non-devolved areas (such as European and international affairs, macroeconomic policy, and social security).

Two approaches will be competing and interacting. The default option is of a replication of characteristically 'Whitehall' and 'Westminster' patterns carried over from the Scottish Office, but innovation to reflect not just Scottish circumstances but also new approaches not previously adopted at British level is also possible. Many civil servants might instinctively prefer the former, but the more forward-thinking might hope that ministers would take the opportunity of devolution to explore departures from Whitehall practice - particularly those derived from organisational models in business.

These decisions will be driven by a mix of organisational and political motivations. Traditionally, most British (and Scottish Office) politicians have not been prominent actors in civil service management, leaving the initiative on the 'brigading' of functions to officials. But in the context of setting up the new administration, these organisational choices will be more visible and have a politically symbolic aspect. Other parties have been given the right to meet the civil service to discuss their organisational ideas on the model of practice before UK General Elections. The first meeting, with the SNP, took place on 21st January 1999. There has inevitably been close continuity between planning the devolution proposals and planning the transition. A majority Labour administration, or one dominated by Labour, might favour a carryover of structure and practice from the Scottish Office. This would be less likely in wider coalition or an Executive without Labour. The management of coalition government is likely to be an important and unprecedented test for the Scottish civil service. Many decisions require to be taken during the transition which will directly affect how officials do their job:

i) the number of ministries

The Scottish Executive has a choice between a Cabinet of free-standing functional ministries which if they covered devolved responsibilities in a conventional way might number 10-12, and a replication of the present structure of the Scottish Office with 5-6 departments. Continuity would suggest the latter, and the devolution minister Henry McLeish is reported as favouring it.

A recent report 'Holistic Government', (1) suggests that it will be difficult to reduce functional departments to below nine, but puts forward its own model of six departments structured around political objectives. Another approach would be to take the present structure of groups and directorates and leave them as relatively free-standing units, combined only loosely. The use of junior ministers is also an important variable. Party manifestos for the May 1999 elections may well develop some innovative answers. A related point is the physical location of ministries. Just as the CSG has suggested that some parliamentary committees should be permanently based outside Edinburgh, it is easy to imagine that parties may propose the dispersal of whole departments to other Scottish locations, going well beyond the present location of industry staff in Glasgow.

ii) central functions

For the civil service there is particular importance for central functions which in the Scottish Office are done on an Office-wide basis.

These include :

- finance - the 'Treasury equivalent'
- establishments and personnel management
- information
- European affairs (recently added in a new division)
- secretariat for ministers and senior officials
- parliamentary liaison
- London liaison.

The interest of the civil service is likely to be in maintaining an integrated central capability in these matters. A particularly important decision facing the Executive is whether it to have its local version of the Treasury responsible for both economic and public expenditure matters and headed by a Scottish Chancellor or Minister of Finance who would become the No 2 to the First Minister. Personnel management and local government finance could also be rolled up in this 'Treasury equivalent'. The decision on this will revolve around a political judgment on whether or not the Executive needs a 'strong Treasury' to enforce expenditure discipline in a context of its limited resource-raising powers.

iii) the First Minister's Office and central policy development

The First Minister is likely to require local versions of the main components of the No 10 Downing Street Office - the Private Office, the Press Office, the Policy Unit and the Political Office. Choices on how far these functions can be combined with the Executive Secretariat will then be required, and how much continuity that will embody from the present Constitution Group, ministerial Private Office, Permanent Secretary's office and Management Group Support Staff.

iv) special advisers and information officers

The Scottish Office has a less well-developed tradition than Whitehall departments of using political or special advisers. Their use has however increased under the Labour Government and there is likely to be pressure from Executive ministers to have their own. This also relates to the question of whether ministers will have their own information officers and/or 'spin doctors', whether or not brought in from outside the Scottish Office.

v) gradings and hierarchies

Pressure within the civil service in recent years has been towards reducing senior posts, a 'delayering' to give middle-ranking officials more responsibility and access, the opening up of posts to those without a conventional civil service background, and individual contracts. All these innovative trends could be accelerated under the Executive, and if wished, it could move radically from the traditional Scottish Office pattern of defining senior posts in terms of a supervisory span over distinct tasks.

vi) working practices

It is not clear how far Scottish officials will replicate the Whitehall/Westminster manner of parliamentary questions, ministerial correspondence, and written and oral evidence to Parliamentary Committees. The CSG report is relatively silent on likely demands on officials but they might be extensive given the numbers of committees. The Committee structure of the Parliament, particularly the handling of financial control through its Finance and Audit Committees, will have a major influence on the approach of the civil service.

vii) liaison with Whitehall

The codification of working arrangements with Whitehall departments in a series of 'concordats' has been a theme of advance planning for devolution. Many of these matters will only work out in the longer term, but interactions arising soon after the handover will be especially important. These are most likely to arise in central services fields like finance and European representation. Relations at official level will reflect the common civil service culture; but when there are sharp political disagreements the advantages to the Scottish Administration of being part of one Home Civil Service may be minimal.

The Scottish Parliament is a double challenge for the civil service. It requires new working mechanisms covering many practical arrangements above and below the level of public awareness. But it also represents a new start for public administration. Two personalities already stand out - Muir Russell, Permanent Secretary of the Scottish Office, and Robert Gordon, head of the Constitution Group and member of the CSG. They presage a new breed of more visible public officials in Scotland as the civil service works out a balance between the traditions and practices it has inherited and the novel political context it will face.

Chapter Nine:
Financial Arrangements

Colin Mair and Barry McCloud

The financing of the Scottish Parliament, and through it the range of public authorities and agencies for which it has devolved responsibility, may seem a rather dry topic. However, as the financial framework will critically impinge on the Parliament's ability to deliver a distinctively Scottish approach to public policy and public services, and the determination of a fair and acceptable level of public spending in Scotland has been seen as one of the potential friction points with Westminster, the topic is of importance.

This chapter provides a straightforward description of financial arrangements proposed, and identifies some of the issues and tensions. It aims to address changes when the Scottish Parliament is inaugurated, and will begin by describing the situation prior to the Parliament sitting.

The Pre-Parliamentary Financial Framework

The planning and control of public expenditure in the UK is based on a rolling three-year plan, updated annually. The first year of the plan is the government's proposals for public spending in the forthcoming year which, balanced by its proposals for taxation and borrowing, effectively form the budget presented to Parliament for that year. These plans are presented annually as 'the government's public spending plans'.

To create the plan, all spending departments of government agree spending totals with the Treasury used for control purposes, and unless some unpredictable eventuality arises these totals will be binding. Within this system, the Scottish Office has responsibility for planning and subsequently controlling spending on all Scottish based public service programmes including local government and the National Health Service. This arrangement has prevailed since the last devolution initiative in 1979. Nationally managed services such as social security and pensions are not the financial responsibility of the Scottish Office although they operate within Scotland.

The vast bulk of the spending allowed in Scotland is funded by a 'block' grant from Westminster, although some is funded by business rate and council tax income generated in Scotland. The Scottish spending limit agreed with the Treasury includes both that funded by the Westminster grant and that funded from business and residential property taxation in Scotland. This means that the Scottish Office has to control and cap local government spending as well as its own direct spending.

Table Seven: Major Recipients of the Block Grant

Support to Local Authorities

Health

Education: Further & Higher

Housing

Roads & Transport

Industry, Enterprise & Training

Law, Order & Protective Services

Agriculture, Fisheries & Food

Provision to Match European Funds

Local Authority Capital

Other Public Services

Other Environmental Services

Source : 'Understanding Grant Distribution', Conferences and Seminars, Edinburgh: COSLA 1996.

These elements of the Scottish Block are all devolved responsibilities of the Scottish Parliament under the Scotland Act. Although the composition is calculated service area by service area, once the total is agreed the Secretary of State has the freedom to allocate it between service areas as seen fit (1).

The Scottish Block is calculated annually in two ways. Where comparable English service areas exist these elements of the Scottish Block are changed annually by the so-called 'Barnett Formula'. Where no comparable English programmes exist, inflation and

demand factors are taken into account. The amount of spending in Scotland subject to the Barnett Formula is 96%. (2)

The Barnett Formula is much misunderstood and often confused with an attempt to apply needs based assessment to the allocation of UK public spending (i.e. to measure the relative need for public services in different parts of the UK and allocate public spending accordingly). Barnett is a population formula introduced after the last attempt of review needs and public spending levels across the UK in 1979. (3) That review by the Treasury found that spending per head on comparable services was 22% higher in Scotland than in England, with only 16% justified by higher levels of need.

The aim of the Barnett Formula was to close that gap by linking increases/decreases in Scottish spending directly to changes in equivalent English budgets on the basis of a population based formula. For example, in any year Scotland would receive increases or decreases in its service budgets based on a pro rata population share of increases/decreases in comparable English budgets. (4) For example, on current weighting the Scottish population is 10.66% of that in England, so Scotland gets 10.66% of equivalent English budgetary increases. For instance, if planned health expenditure in England is increased by £1 billion, the Scottish Budget is increased by £106.6 million. As Barnett applied only to budget increases or decreases on an annual basis, not the whole budget, then it was recognised that Scotland's historical advantage would continue for a long period, as it has to date. The population formula was updated in 1992 as new census data become available.

No attempt has been made since the 1970s to review the link between all public service spending and social need across the whole UK. However, a report commissioned by the Scottish Office in 1997 on relative local government spending found that even adjusting for differences in responsibilities and demand, Scottish spending on local services was 18% per capita higher than in England. (5) Identifiable government expenditure in Scotland was 19% higher than for the UK as a whole, although this aggregate figure hides massive variations between expenditure programmes, as Table Eight shows.

Table Eight: Identifiable General Government Expenditure per head by Programme in Scotland 1996-97

Scotland relative to the UK UK = 100	
Agriculture, fisheries, food and forestry	85
Trade, industry, energy, employment and training	139
Transport	127
Housing	162
Other environmental services	144
Law, order and protective services	101
Education	126
Culture, media and sport	103
Health and personal social services	119
Social security	109
Total	119

Source: 'Government Expenditure and Revenue in Scotland 1996-1997', Edinburgh: The Scottish Office 1997.

To sum up, the financial framework prior to the Parliament has incorporated the following major elements :

- An annual limit on the total spending of Scottish based public services, including spending undertaken by local government.

- Permitted spending funded by block grant from Westminster, augmented by council tax and business rate income.

- Uprating of the Scottish block annually by applying a population based formula (Barnett) to increases or decreases in comparable English service budgets. No attempt has been made to link total spending in Scotland, England, Wales and Ireland to measures of social need.

- Additional allocations outwith the block to meet unforeseen eventualities, e.g. natural or civil disasters, or on the basis of government decisions applying to the whole of the UK (e.g. to meet the cost of pay increases nationally agreed).

The Scottish Parliament

Perhaps surprisingly, given the importance of the constitutional change, the financial system changes relatively little with the new Parliament. The major change is that decisions about the use of spending permitted in Scotland will be taken by an elected Parliament in Edinburgh rather than by Ministers appointed in Westminster. However, the Parliament will make these decisions within the context of the pre-existing public expenditure framework, with one major change.

The UK Government's public spending plans will continue to set the limit on all spending devolved to the Parliament. The block grant from Westminster will continue to be uprated annually by the Barnett Formula, although this has no legal status and can be changed if Westminster so wishes. Local government spending funded by the business rate and council tax will still be planned and controlled within the Parliament's spending total.

The major change is that the Parliament has a tax power previously not available to the Scottish Office, and the power to vary the standard rate of income tax up or down by three-pence-in-the pound. It is estimated that the full use of the power to vary up would raise around £450 million, (6) which is relatively small beer against the block grant of over £14 billion. It was strongly argued that this power was essential to the credibility of the Parliament as otherwise it would have no more financial capacity than the Scottish Office that was simply a department of the UK Government. However, the Labour Party has already indicated it will not use this power in Scottish Parliament's first term.

The tax-varying power does give the Parliament a modest financing capacity independent of Westminster but its use is potentially a very double-edged sword. If the Scottish population is able to pay more in income tax than the rest of the UK then why should Westminster provide greater financial support for public services in Scotland than it does in England? Given the Barnett Formula is a convention, not law, and no assessment of relative need has taken place since 1977, then use of the tax power may bring Scotland's relatively higher spending into question.

Key Issues in the Financial Arrangements

As noted, with the exception of monies raised by using the tax varying power, the Parliament's spending will continue to be planned and controlled within the UK public expenditure planning process. The Parliament will therefore operate for its first three years within spending plans and limits already published by the government for 1999/2000-2001/20027. These plans have the government's priorities built into them, and although the Parliament can vary spending within the limits set, it will be unable to exceed these limits without using the tax varying power. There is clearly a potential tension between the Parliament's devolved responsibility for major areas of public policy, and the fact that its spending capacity is largely pre-determined by Westminster. Furthermore, expectations raised by the creation of the Parliament may sit uneasily with its restricted financial capacity. The Prime Minister's remark that the Parliament has no more independent financial capacity than an English Parish Council, while misjudged, may nevertheless express a sense of constraint that will require careful management.

This problem will not exist solely at the outset but will recur through annually negotiated expenditure plans. At present these are negotiations between departments of the UK Government in Westminster, but once the Parliament sits they will become significantly more politicised, particularly if the administration in the Scottish Parliament is of a different political persuasion than the UK government. Unless carefully handled, there is an inbuilt risk that these negotiations will focus on a Scotland versus the UK form of politics. Equally, if devolution, as some have suggested, creates an English backlash the basis for Scotland's higher level of spending per capita may come under scrutiny.

As noted above, there has been no review of social needs and public spending across the UK since 1979, Scotland's spending per capita on territorially comparable service areas is almost 20% higher than the UK average and the Barnett Formula that was supposed to bring greater convergence in spending has not achieved this. While clearly issues of population sparcity, social need and service standards can be invoked to justify Scotland's higher spending, the fact remains that there is no recent detailed needs analysis to support these claims.

The Treasury Select Committee in Westminster has concurred with the Treasury view that resources should be allocated according to need and that the territorial allocation of public spending in the UK needs objectively reviewed and adjusted if necessary.

This is sometimes represented as a review of the Barnett Formula, but as noted above Barnett determines the annual uprating of Scottish service budgets in line with comparable English budgets; it does not determine the core budgets being updated. A review of needs and spending would be much more fundamental as it would question the core budgets themselves. The outcome of any such review cannot be specified in advance but it would be unlikely to sustain Scotland's share if the needs indicators used in the 1979 Treasury Report were updated. The tax-varying power may be an issue here as a reduction of funding from Westminster might be justified on the basis that if Scotland wants higher spending it should be paid for by higher taxation in Scotland itself not from the UK Treasury.

The Barnett Formula itself is open to review as the population figures used have been updated only once since its introduction, and Scotland's share of the UK population is falling annually. The next census in 2001 will produce a comprehensive database for uprating the population base for Barnett, and that would potentially have an impact from 2002 onwards in reducing the Scottish Block.

Clearly, this is a political and not merely a technical matter, and if demonstrating the benefits of the union to Scotland remains important, political considerations are likely to be critical in determining the Parliament's spending power. Sharp reductions would certainly fuel current debates about Scotland's contribution to UK revenues through North Sea Oil, and raises issues about England's allegedly disproportionate share of spending that is not territorially identified (e.g. defence procurement; motorways etc). Again, as with other aspects of the Parliament, its political composition and political relationship with Westminster will be critical to how the financial arrangements operate.

The final issue is the Parliament's relationship with local government which will be directly influenced by the Parliament's financial arrangements. As spending by local government that it finances itself through council tax remains within the spending limit set for the Parliament, then the Parliament will have to adopt mechanisms to control local spending. Such control is potentially at odds with concepts of subsidiarity, decentralisation and local democracy inherent in the case for the Parliament itself and may create a recurrent friction over local spending limits. The problem for the Parliament will be that if local government spending was not controlled, other areas of spending such as the health service would have to be squeezed to remain within the spending limit.

In conclusion, the financial arrangements for the Parliament are inherent in its status as a subordinate rather than sovereign body. It remains part of, and subject to, the UK expenditure planning and control system, and the tax varying power gives only limited financial discretion. Depending on its composition and the management of political relations with Westminster this may become a source of friction and instability. It also raises questions of accountability as the Parliament has very limited independent financial capacity, and a temptation may be to blame Westminster for frustrating Scottish aspirations. A high level of political maturity and tolerance on all sides will be necessary to make the arrangement work well, but this is true for all elements of the devolution project.

Chapter Ten:
The Scottish Legal System

Sarah O'Neill

The Scottish legal system is unique and distinct from that of the rest of the United Kingdom. Following the Treaty of Union of the Parliaments of Scotland and England in 1707, the laws and legal institutions of Scotland and of England and Wales were not merged, but remained separate. Scots law has evolved to become markedly different from that of England and Wales. Its origins are in European legal systems derived from Roman law, as opposed to England and Wales, which takes a common law approach.

The present system - sources and types of Scots law

There are three main sources of Scots law. The first two sources, judge-made law (also known as precedent or caselaw), and institutional writings (certain authoritative legal writings), are together generally referred to as the common law of Scotland. The third, and perhaps most important, is legislation. Legislation consists of statutes (Acts of Parliament), subordinate legislation authorised by Parliament (mainly rules and regulations made by Ministers/ government departments), and European Union legislation. (1)

Scots law divides into two main branches, civil and criminal law.

- Civil law decides disputes between two parties, whether individuals, administrative authorities or commercial organisations. Civil law can be separated into two parts - public and private law.

- Public law regulates and controls political and administrative power within the state. It concerns the activities of Parliament, the courts, central and local government, and public bodies, for example the regulators of private utilities, such as Ofgas and Offer, and their relationships with private individuals. Public law provides mechanisms to challenge the decisions made by such bodies, such as judicial review (2) and tribunals.

- Private law deals with the rights and obligations of citizens between themselves. The main areas of private law are family law (dealing with marriage, divorce, residence and contact with children, guardianship and adoption), the law of contract, the law of delict (which deals mainly with civil wrongs for which the wrongdoer must pay compensation, such as defamation, damage to property or personal injury caused by negligence), and the law of property.

- Criminal law is where the state prosecutes alleged criminal activity. (3) Rather than relationships between individuals or organisations, criminal law is concerned with maintaining the peace and order of the community, and the prosecution and punishment of crime.

The remainder of this chapter looks at how the Scottish Parliament's powers to make its own legislation will change the Scottish legal system. It also considers new powers which the Scotland Act gives the courts, and the procedures it introduces for appointing and removing judges.

1. The powers of the Scottish Parliament to make legislation

Since 1707, Scotland, as well as England and Wales, has been governed by the laws of the United Kingdom Parliament. Under the doctrine of sovereignty of Parliament, Acts of Parliament are absolutely binding on all courts, taking precedence over all other sources of law including the common law, except European Union law. However, the Treaty of Union contains safeguards for Scots private law and the Scottish court system.

Given the status of the Scottish legal system within the UK, there are particular arrangements at Westminster for handling the progress of Scottish legislation. The Secretary of State for Scotland has overall responsibility for the Scottish legal system, while the Lord Advocate (4) is responsible for the drafting of Scottish legislation.

At present, legislation relating to Scots private law and most of that relating to the criminal law in Scotland is purely Scottish. However, currently this legislation must be enacted by the Westminster Parliament, during time allotted in the parliamentary timetable. Thus, under the present system, although Scotland has its own law and legal system, it has no legislative body of its own to amend and update its laws

Many other areas of the law in Scotland are largely regulated by statutory provisions which apply to the entire UK. Examples include the law relating to employment, companies, social security and consumer protection. Many of these areas have also in recent years become increasingly regulated by European law.

The Scotland Act will alter the Scottish situation significantly. It provides that, within its legislative competence (ie. in relation to matters which are devolved), the Parliament may make laws, to be known as Acts of the Scottish Parliament. However, it is made clear that the Westminster Parliament will remain sovereign. (5)

Subject to the list of reserved matters contained in the Act, the Scottish Parliament will have power to legislate on both the civil and the criminal law in Scotland. Reserved matters include the constitution, employment, companies, social security and consumer protection, which will continue to be within the powers of the Westminster Parliament.

2. Devolution issues and the powers of the courts

While the Scotland Act gives the Scottish Parliament power to make laws on devolved matters, Westminster retains its sovereignty. Accordingly, the Scottish Parliament must act only within the powers given by the Act, and it can only pass laws in relation to matters within its legislative competence.

The Act contains provisions for resolving devolution issues, (7) which may arise where there is a dispute as to whether a specific matter is within the legislative competence of the Scottish Parliament. There are various mechanisms in the Act to ensure that such issues are resolved insofar as possible before a Bill is introduced into Parliament. These are explained in more detail in Chapter Fourteen.

However, should a devolution issue arise at a later stage, the Scotland Act provides that an Act of the Scottish Parliament, or the actions of Ministers, may be challenged in the courts on the grounds that such Acts or actions are outwith the legislative competence of the Parliament.

It is likely that any devolution issues which arise at this stage will occur in one of the following situations:-

- where an individual or other body wishes to challenge outright the validity of an Act of Parliament, subordinate legislation or an administrative action

- where, in the course of a litigation or prosecution, one party is relying on a piece of legislation or an administrative act which the other party wishes to challenge as invalid.

Devolution issues, which the courts may be asked to rule upon, are defined in the Act, (8) as questions as to whether :

- an Act or subordinate legislation is within the legislative competence of the Scottish Parliament.

- any function which any person purports or proposes to exercise, is a function of the Scottish Ministers, the First Minister or the Lord Advocate.

- the purported or proposed exercise of a function by a member of the Scottish Executive is within devolved competence.

- a member of the Scottish Executive purports or proposes to exercise a function, incompatible with rights under the European Convention of Human Rights or with European Community Law.

- a failure to act by a member of the Scottish Executive would be incompatible with rights under the European Convention of Human Rights or with European Community Law.

- a function is exercisable within devolved competence or in or as regards Scotland.

- any other question arising under the Act about reserved matters.

Proceedings relating to devolution issues may be raised in courts in Scotland, England and Wales, or Northern Ireland. In Scotland, proceedings may be brought by the Lord Advocate or Advocate General, but may also be raised by any other person. In civil and criminal cases, a court or tribunal may refer the issue to the Court of Session, or the High Court of Justiciary.

If necessary, either of these courts may refer the case to the Judicial Committee of the Privy Council. (9) Any appeal against the determination of a devolution issue will also go to the Judicial Committee. (10)

3. Judges

The primary function of judges is to determine disputes between two parties. Judges must apply the law and follow statute, and in interpreting statutes and applying existing caselaw, also make law. The terms of the Scotland Act add a further, extremely significant, dimension to the role of judges in Scotland. As we have seen, Acts of the Scottish Parliament and the actions of the Executive will be open to challenge in the courts. As a result, in addition to their existing roles, judges will now be required to adjudicate on constitutional matters.

The independence of the judiciary has always been a fundamental element of the unwritten UK constitution. If judges are to perform their functions adequately, they must be free from political influence, particularly in their appointment. Given the new constitutional powers given by the Scotland Act, it will be more important than ever that judges retain their independence.

The procedures for appointment and removal of judges in Scotland have been a matter of controversy, partly due to concerns regarding political influence, and perhaps partly because the existing procedures might be viewed as secretive and lacking in accountability. The Act goes some way towards addressing these concerns, by introducing new procedures for the appointment and removal of judges. These were the subject of considerable debate during the passing of the Scotland Bill.

The current system for appointment and removal of judges and sheriffs is as follows:

1. Judges of the Court of Session (who also sit in the criminal High Court of Justiciary) are the senior permanent judges. They are appointed by the Sovereign, (11) after nomination by the Secretary of State on the recommendation of the Lord Advocate. Those appointed prior to March 31st 1995 must retire at the age of 75. Those appointed after that date must retire at age 70, but can sit as retired judges until age 75.

   Under common law, judges can be removed only on grounds of misconduct. (12) However, there is at present no particular mechanism for removal of a Scottish judge from office. (13)

2. Sheriffs (14) sit in the local sheriff courts, which have a very wide jurisdiction, both civil and criminal. Sheriffs are appointed by the Sovereign, on the nomination of the Lord Advocate. Sheriffs appointed prior to March 31st 1995 must retire at the age of 72. Those appointed after that date must retire at the age of 70.

Sheriffs can be removed from office. If, after investigation by the Lord President and the Lord Justice-Clerk, a sheriff is reported as unfit for office 'by reason of inability, neglect of duty, or misbehaviour' the Secretary of State may make a statutory instrument (subject to annulment by Parliament) removing him or her. This happens very rarely.

The new procedures introduced by the Scotland Act are outlined below:

Appointment: The First Minister, after consulting with the Lord President, is to recommend the appointment of a person as a judge of the Court of Session, a sheriff principal or a sheriff. (15) However, before such a recommendation is made, the person must first be nominated by the First Minister. Before nominating them, the First Minister must consult the Lord President and the Lord Justice Clerk. (16)

Removal: The Act provides a procedure for the removal of a Court of Session judge. A judge may be removed from office only by the Queen, on the recommendation of the First Minister.

The First Minster may make such a recommendation only in the following circumstances:-

- The First Minister must constitute a tribunal to investigate and report on whether a judge of the Court of Session is unfit for office by reason of 'inability, neglect of duty or misbehaviour'.

- The report received from the tribunal by the First Minister concludes that the judge is unfit for office by reason of inability, neglect of duty or misbehaviour, and gives reasons for that conclusion.

- On the basis of this report, which must then be laid before the Parliament, the First Minister makes a motion for the removal of the judge from office.

- The Parliament resolves, on the motion of the First Minister, that the judge should be removed.

Conclusion

This chapter has given a brief outline of changes which the establishment of a Scottish Parliament will bring for the Scottish legal system. It is clear that, although Scotland had always had its own separate legal system, the advent of the Scottish Parliament will bring significant changes to the way in which law is enacted in Scotland and will give Scottish judges a very clear role in the new constitutional arrangements.

Chapter Eleven: The New Electoral System

Andy Myles

The electoral system to be used for Scottish Parliament elections is a variant of the Additional Member System (AMS) of proportional representation systems, the best known of which is used in Germany. In Scotland it arrived via the negotiations inside the Constitutional Convention where its principle elements were said to be:

- easy for the voter used to First-Past-the-Post (FPTP) to understand
- linked MSPs to a geographic area
- provided a broadly proportional result.

The First, Constituency Ballot Paper

Voters will be given two ballot papers. The first will be for their own parliamentary constituency, which will be the same as those for Westminster (except for Orkney & Shetland where there will be one Scottish Constituency for each). This ballot will use FPTP voting as currently used for Westminster. Thus, the first 73 MSPs will be elected using a very familiar method; the MSPs will have a definite constituency; but the overall result would be as lacking in proportionality as the results of the current Westminster electoral arrangements if these were the only MSPs.

The Second, List Ballot Paper

The purpose of this second ballot will be to broadly correct the lack of proportionality from the first ballot. Voters will be given a second paper and indicate their preferred party (thus achieving the aim of simplicity). Each party on the ballot paper will be represented by a list of candidates and from these lists will be drawn the 56 Additional Members, allocated by a mathematical formula designed to ensure the proportionate correction.

In order to retain a geographic link for the list candidates, Scotland will be divided into eight regions (initially based on the old European Parliamentary constituencies) and seven Additional Members elected from each.

Using the Second Ballot to Correct the First Ballot

The way in which the correction will be done is as follows :

1. The first, constituency ballots will be counted using FPTP and 73 winners declared.

2. The number of votes cast for each party in the second, list ballot will be counted.

3. The list ballot total of votes for each party will then be divided by the number of constituency MSPs gained by that party in the constituencies, contained within that region, plus one.

4. The party with the highest total after the calculation above has been done gains the first Additional Member.

5. The second to seventh Additional Members are allocated in the same way, but at each stage the Additional Members already elected for each party are added to constituency members elected for that party plus one, before the division. (The same total party vote is used at each stage.)

The effect of this formula is to reflect the second vote rather than the first in the final outcome. It is also likely to mean that if a party gets over 6% of the votes in a region and wins no constituency MSPs it would probably see the top candidate on its list elected as an Additional Member. On current voting patterns it is likely, therefore, that the four existing major parties in Scotland have a good chance of seeing candidates elected in all eight regions. Smaller parties are also offered some hope by this effect, although there is, in effect, a higher hurdle to be crossed than the 5% formal bar in the German system.

Using this system, calculations have been done to show that, on the basis of the votes cast at Westminster general elections, a broadly proportional result would have resulted (and no party would have gained an outright majority) in every election since 1974. (Earlier elections are difficult to assess as the Liberal or Nationalist parties put forward only limited numbers of candidates). There are, however, complicating factors. Voters will not be bound to vote for candidates of the same parties on both ballot papers. In a recent election in New Zealand, using a very similar system, 38% of voters 'cross-voted'.

There is strong evidence to suggest that throughout the years of Conservative Government, a significant minority of non-Tory voters in Scotland have developed the habit of tactical voting under the FPTP system, and this might well translate into cross-voting under the new AMS voting. Such cross-voting would have the effect of altering the allocations of Additional Members, but should still produce a result broadly proportional to the list ballot totals. AMS certainly represents an advance from first-past-the-post in terms of voter choice.

So what are the likely consequences for Scottish politics of the use of a proportional electoral system? The direct answer is that we may enter an era of coalition politics. The experience of other countries using PR is that coalition government has become the norm. This means that a huge shift will be witnessed, away from a two party, confrontational model to a multi-party, competitive model. How Scotland copes with coalition building depends greatly on the stability of the system and the parties, and the developing political environment within Scotland. It is here that the major changes inherent in proportionality may have most effect.

The indirect answer to the question as to the effect of a proportional system is that it will change the environment and dynamics of politics. Scotland has, for over a century of democratic politics seen the hegemony of one party - first the Liberals and then Labour - but always much more a function of the electoral system than the way people voted. Ironically, the only political party to win over 50% of the votes at a general election in post-war Scotland has been the Conservatives in 1955. (1) But under a PR system all of the parties are likely to be minority parties. All of the parties will be potential coalition partners - almost all of the time. The power and patronage that go with hegemony will be spread. The closed politics that come of one party monopolising power will become more open. The psychology of dominance will go - particularly if proportional representation comes to local government.

The First Elections: The Battlegrounds

The first Scottish Parliament elections will be fought on two electoral battlefronts - one, the FPTP constituencies familar to Westminster elections and second, the eight regional AMS constituences. Tables Nine and Ten highlight the marginal FPTP battleground all the parties must face in a four party system, while Figure One shows the relative strengths of the parties in the AMS regional seats.

Looking at the parties marginal and target seats, Labour's most marginal seats emphasise the high point of 1997 for the party's electoral fortunes - with seven of the ten seats being gains in the 1997 general election and further gains unlikely. The SNP's target seats reveals the lack of Labour-SNP marginals despite this being the national competition which defines Scottish politics - with only five Labour seats having majorities over the SNP of 20% or under.

The Conservatives top target seats illustrate the decline of the Tories - with all their top ten targets being ex-Tory seats eight of which were lost in 1997. An important benchmark for the Tories in the Scottish Parliament elections will be whether they win or can come close in any of their ex-FPTP seats. The Liberal Democrats paucity of target seats with the exception of Aberdeen South illustrates that their vote is effectively concentrated in the FPTP seats they currently hold and any further gains look highly unlikely.

The eight regional seats reveal on 1997 voting patterns the distinct party contests in different parts of Scotland and the fact that Scotland has always had a more complex political system than simple Labour dominance. The West of Scotland-Glasgow region (including the geographically mistitled Central Scotland) has a formidable Labour hegemony, whereas Mid-Scotland and Lothians has a weaker Labour hold and in places a strong SNP challenge, and the Highlands and Islands and North East a competitive four party system.

The Scottish political process will be changed by the establishment of the Parliament and new electoral system. (2) The established parties will change in character, organisation and policy development, (3) while new parties and alliances may arise and win support and votes.

Table Nine: Scottish Political Parties Most Marginal Seats

	% Maj.	Second Party
Ten Most Marginal Labour Seats		
1. Inverness East, Nairn and Lochaber	4.9	SNP
2. Eastwood	6.2	Con
3. Aberdeen South	7.6	Lib Dem
4. Glasgow Govan	9.0	SNP
5. Ochil	10.6	SNP
6. Edinburgh Pentlands	10.6	Con
7. Ayr	14.6	Con
8. Stirling	14.9	Con
9. Kilmarnock and Loudoun	15.3	SNP
10. Dumfries	19.5	Con
Ten Most Marginal Liberal Democrat Seats		
1. Tweedale, Ettrick and Lauderdale	3.8	Lab
2. Aberdeenshire West and Kincardine	6.2	Con
3. Caithness, Sutherland and Easter Ross	7.7	Lab
4. Ross, Skye and Inverness West	10.1	Lab
5. Edinburgh West	15.2	Con
6. Gordon	16.6	Con
7. Argyll and Bute	17.0	SNP
8. Roxburgh and Berwickshire	22.6	Con
9. Fife North East	24.7	Lab
10. = Orkney *	33.7	Lab
10. = Shetland*	33.7	Lab
Six Most Marginal SNP Seats		
1. Perth	7.1	Con
2. Tayside North	9.1	Con
3. Galloway and Upper Nithsdale	13.4	Con
4. Moray	14.0	Con
5. Angus	23.6	Con
6. Banff and Buchan	31.9	Con

* Figures based on Orkney and Shetland 1997 general election result.

Table Ten: Scottish Political Parties Target Seats

	% Behind	Winning Party
Five Labour Target Seats		
1. Tweedale, Ettrick and Lauderdale	3.8	Lib Dem
2. Caithness, Sutherland and Easter Ross	7.7	Lib Dem
3. Ross, Skye and Inverness West	10.1	Lib Dem
4. Perth	11.6	SNP
5. Moray	21.7	SNP
Ten SNP Target Seats		
1. Inverness East, Nairn and Lochaber	4.9	Lab
2. Glasgow Govan	9.0	Lab
3. Ochil	10.6	Lab
4. Caithness, Sutherland and Easter Ross	12.5	Lib Dem
5. Tweedale, Ettrick and Lauderdale	14.1	Lib Dem
6. Kilmarnock and Loudoun	15.3	Lab
7. Argull and Bute	17.0	Lib Dem
8. Ross, Skye and Inverness West	19.1	Lib Dem
9. Renfrewshire West	20.0	Lab
10. Western Isles	22.2	Lab
Ten Conservative Target Seats		
1. Aberdeenshire West and Kincardine	6.2	Lib Dem
2. Eastwood	6.2	Lab
3. Perth	7.1	SNP
4. Aberdeen South	8.9	Lab
5. Tweedale, Ettrick and Lauderdale	9.1	Lib Dem
6. Edinburgh Pentlands	10.6	Lab
7. Galloway and Upper Nithsdale	13.4	SNP
8. Moray	14.0	SNP
9. Ayr	14.6	Lab
10. Stirling	14.9	Lab
Five Liberal Democrat Target Seats		
1. Aberdeen South	7.6	Lib Dem
2. Inverness East, Nairn and Lochaber	16.4	Lab
3. Eastwood	28.0	Lab
4. Perth	28.4	SNP
5. Edinburgh South	29.2	Lab

FIG. ONE: SCOTTISH PARLIAMENTARY ELECTION RESULT:
Notional figures on 1997 General Election voting results

HIGHLANDS				
	% share of vote	FPTP	AMS	Total. No of Seats
Lib Dem	27.7	5	0	5
Lab	27.0	2	2	4
SNP	26.7	1	3	4
Con	16.2	0	2	2

NORTH EAST SCOTLAND				
	% share of vote	FPTP	AMS	Total. No of Seats
Lab	30.9	5	0	5
SNP	26.1	2	2	4
Con	22.4	0	4	4
Lib Dem	18.9	2	1	3

MID-SCOTLAND AND FIFE				
	% share of vote	FPTP	AMS	Total. No of Seats
Lab	40.0	6	1	7
SNP	25.3	2	2	4
Con	21.1	0	3	3
Lib Dem	12.6	1	1	2

GLASGOW				
	% share of vote	FPTP	AMS	Total. No of Seats
Lab	60.4	10	2	12
SN P	19.2	0	3	3
Con	8.5	0	1	1
Lib Dem	7.3	0	1	1

CENTRAL SCOTLAND

	% share of vote	FPTP	AMS	Total. No of Seats
Lab	59.3	10	1	11
SN P	23.4	0	4	4
Con	10.4	0	2	2
Lib Dem	5.2	0	0	0

WEST OF SCOTLAND

	% share of vote	FPTP	AMS	Total. No of Seats
Lab	51.3	9	0	9
S N P	19.9	0	3	3
Con	18.2	0	3	3
Lib Dem	9.2	0	1	1

LOTHIANS

	% share of vote	FPTP	AMS	Total. No of Seats
Lab	45.9	8	0	8
Con	19.2	0	3	3
SNP	18.4	0	3	3
Lib Dem	14.9	1	1	2

SOUTH OF SCOTLAND

	% share of vote	FPTP	AMS	Total. No of Seats
Lab	43.4	6	1	7
Con	22.6	0	4	4
SNP	19.1	1	2	3
Lib Dem	13.4	2	0	2

TOTALS

	% share of vote	FPTP	AMS	Total. No of Seats
Lab	45.6	56	7	63
SN P	22.1	6	22	28
Con	17.5	0	22	22
Lib Dem	13.0	11	5	16

Source:
John Curtice,
Dept of Government,
Strathclyde University

Chapter Twelve:
Relations with Other Public Bodies

Brian Hogwood

This section is concerned with the Scottish Parliament's relations with public bodies. These bodies, other than departments of the Executive and their agencies, Scottish local government, and the European Union, include both purely Scottish non-departmental public bodies (sometimes loosely referred to as 'quangos') reporting to the Scottish Parliament through the Executive, and cross-border public bodies. Ironically, the Scotland Act has far more to say about cross-border bodies than those coming only under the Scottish Parliament.

This section considers what the terms non-departmental public body and quango can mean; quantifies the significance of public bodies in terms of their number, staffing and finance; sets out how the public body universe in Scotland has been transformed since 1979, when devolution was last seriously considered, and sets out key issues in the relationship between the Scottish Parliament and public bodies.

What are non-departmental Public Bodies?

The term 'non-departmental public body' (NDPB) was first used in the Pliatzky Report published in January 1980. This was commissioned by Margaret Thatcher to investigate the scope of activity of such bodies in the context of their perceived growth, and to make recommendations for reducing their number. (1) The term includes not only the executive bodies with which this section is primarily concerned, but advisory bodies and tribunals which account for the overwhelming majority of appointees. However, it excludes nationalised industries, certain other public corporations (like the BBC), the National Health Service, and a wide range of nominally private, often more locally-based, organisations contracted

to deliver public services.

The term 'quango', though widely used, has been used to cover everything from major national bodies to individual housing associations, or even individual grant-maintained schools. It is sometimes used in a pejorative manner, signalling disapproval of the existence of such bodies, how appointments are made to their boards, or their perceived lack of accountability. (2)

By far the best source for basic information and contact points for non-departmental public bodies in Scotland and elsewhere in Britain is the annual Public Bodies. (3) This provides summary information about number of bodies, staffing and expenditure by department, as well as varying amounts of information about individual organisations (or types of organisation), including the number of appointees and their pay (the answer, even for executive bodies, is often nothing). Some very basic summary information has been provided since 1997 on 'local public spending bodies', such as further and higher education institutions, local enterprise companies, and registered housing associations, whose boards are not appointed by ministers but are to a large extent funded, often indirectly, by public money.

This section will focus primarily on executive non-departmental public bodies (NDPBs), but will refer to the implications for other forms of public body in relation to issues which cut across the categories.

What is the scale of NDPB activity in Scotland?

Findings about the scale of NDPB activity in Scotland depend on coverage and indicators used. Table Eleven shows the implications of including different categories. Table Twelve shows various indicators of the scale of executive NDPB activity. The scope of NDPB activity will be extended shortly before the elections to the Scottish Parliament when responsibility for allocating funding to further education colleges is transferred from the Scottish Office to a newly formed Scottish Further Education Council.

Table Eleven: The Numbers of Scottish Public Bodies 1998

Type	No of Bodies
Executive NDPBs	36
Advisory NDPBs	62
Tribunal NDPBs (sets of)	5
Nat. Industries	3
Other Public Corporations	3
NHS bodies	68
Local spending bodies:	
Higher education	20
Further education	43
Grant maintained schools	2
Local enterprise companies	22
Housing associations	259

Source: Calculated from 'Public Bodies', London: Stationery Office 1998.

Table Twelve: Executive NDPB Activity in Scotland 1997/98

Bodies	Staff	Expenditure £m	Funded by govt £m
36	8,000	1,960	1,650

Executive NDPBs vary enormously in terms of scale and significance, from the Scottish Higher Education Funding Council with expenditure of £552m, to Scottish Conveyancing and Executry Services Board with expenditure of £0.1m.

Table Thirteen: Public Bodies in relation to Scottish Public Sector

	Staff (000s)	Direct expenditure* (£bn)	Funded by Scottish Office (£bn)
Total Scottish Departments	12	2.37	-
-FE	12	2.08	-
National Health Service	101	4.62	4.52
Executive NDPBs	8	1.96	1.65
+FE	8	2.25	1.94
Local government	297	6.52	5.26
Public corporations	-	-	0.61

Note: * Financial year 1997/98. For Scottish Office excludes money passed on to other categories. Sources: Scottish Office Web Site (www.scotland.gov.uk); Cabinet Office, 'Public Bodies' 1998, London: Stationery Office 1998.

Another way of looking at the scale of public body activity is in relation to the total activities for which the Scottish Executive and Parliament are ultimately responsible. Table Thirteen shows NDPB activity in relation to that of the Scottish departments, the National Health Service, and local government. Once account is taken of the transfer of further education expenditure in April 1999, the Scottish Executive departments will have responsibility for less direct expenditure than executive NDPBs, though they in turn are dwarfed by the staffing and expenditure of NHS bodies and local government.

The composition of public body activity has undergone a major transformation since 1979. There were then 84 executive NDPBs, compared to only 36 in 1998. Part of the reason for the decline is the disappearance of whole categories of body. New Town Development Corporations were wound up. Central (educational) Institutions and Colleges of Education, while subject to some termination, largely survived as 'independent corporations', and now fall in the local spending body category.

In the opposite direction, much of the administrative devolution to Scotland since 1979 was administered by NDPBs, either 'new' ones, such as the Scottish Higher Education Funding Council or major new tasks being giving to existing bodies, resulting in their transformation, such as the Special Scottish Housing Association taking on the functions of the Housing Corporation in Scotland and becoming Scottish Homes. (4) The Scottish functions of the Training Agency were added to the Scottish Development Agency, but the result was a new network of a slimmed down Scottish Enterprise and 'private' Local Enterprise Companies (LECs) contracted to provide services, with similar arrangements in the Highlands and Islands. The overall shift has been from a larger number of executive NDPBs often directly involved in service delivery, to a smaller number of often 'money-shifting' bodies, acting as intermediaries between Scottish departments and bodies contracted to supply services.

So far, discussion has been in terms of bodies with a Scottish remit which will come under the Scottish Parliament. However, even with the administrative devolution referred to above there will continue to be a wide range of bodies whose operations affect Scotland, including some falling within the jurisdiction of the Scottish Parliament. Examples cited in the Scotland's Parliament White Paper include the UK Sports Council, the Central Council for Education and Training in Social Work, and the Criminal Injuries Compensation Authority. (5) One important proposed new body falling in this category is the Food Standards Agency. It is important to distinguish between 'umbrella' bodies, like the UK Sports Council, which provide an additional co-ordinating layer on top of councils for each of the component countries, and those like the Criminal Injuries Compensation Authority, which directly deliver services in Scotland and other parts of Britain.

Some of the most interesting cross-border bodies are civil service staffed bodies rather than NDPBs. A prime example is the Forestry Commission, based in Edinburgh but covering all of Great Britain, which has its own separate civil service, and in which Scotland unusually has taken the lead role. There are no available data on the scale of operations of these UK/GB bodies in Scotland. The existence of these cross-border bodies raises questions under many of the issues to which we now turn.

Key Issues in the relationship between the Scottish Parliament and Public Bodies

When the Scottish Parliament and Scottish Executive come into operation, the structure and activities of public bodies in Scotland will be exactly as they were prior to devolution. The Scotland Act itself brings about no changes to their status or coverage, and the Act is largely silent about public bodies, other than in the important area of cross-border bodies. It will subsequently be open to the Scottish Parliament to pass general or specific legislation to alter the inherited pattern, but since most executive NDPBs have a statutory basis, both ad hoc and systemic reforms are likely to be time-consuming.

The crucial point is that the functions of the Scottish Office in relation to NDPBs are inherited not directly by the Scottish Parliament but by the departments of the Scottish Executive. This is made quite explicit in the White Paper:

> *'The Scottish Executive will have responsibility for all Scottish public bodies whose functions and services will be devolved, and will be accountable to the Scottish Parliament for them. The Scottish Executive will assume the responsibilities of Ministers of the Crown in relation to these bodies'. (6)*

These responsibilities include, of course, those of making appointments and proposing funding. As with so many aspects of devolution, what being accountable to the Scottish Parliament means in practice depends very much on the political relationship between MSPs, particularly those in the party or parties forming the Executive, and the leadership in the Executive itself. This could range from Parliament simply being notified of the decisions of the Executive in relation to public bodies, to MSPs (either collectively or only those in the governing parties) requiring prior clearance of all decisions about appointments, guidance etc. The final report of the Consultative Steering Group (CSG) of the Parliament is silent on the role of Parliament in relation to public bodies. (7)

Issues in the relationship between public bodies and the Scottish Parliament can be grouped under the following:

- Appointments
- Scrutiny and accountability of Scottish and cross-border bodies

- 'Patriation' of the Scottish activities of bodies with a UK/GB remit
- Reviewing whether public bodies are the appropriate way to deliver public services.

Appointments

The scale of the task of Parliament in scrutinising appointments will, again, depend on the range of bodies covered. Table Fourteen indicates the numbers of appointments involved for each category. The table does not include the relatively small number of appointments which Scottish Ministers will make to cross-border bodies. The scale of the tasks involved in finding and vetting candidates and in scrutinising the process is obvious.

Table Fourteen: Numbers of Appointments to Scottish Bodies 1998

Type	No. of appointments
Executive NDPBs	434
Advisory NDPBs	580
Tribunal NDPBs	2308
Nationalised Industries	19
Other Public Corporations	32
NHS bodies	436
Total of above	**3809**
of which by ministers	**3652**
Local public spending bodies	
Higher education institutions*	500
Further education institutions*	860
Grant maintained schools*	36
Local Enterprise Companies*	264
Registered Housing Associations*	3108
Total local spending bodies	**4768**

Note: * Official guesstimate. Source: Calculated from 'Public Bodies' 1998, London: Stationery Office.

There are two main routes through which Parliament could be involved in scrutinising appointments. The first is through ensuring that proper procedures, including those concerned with propriety, are being followed. The second would directly involve Parliament in vetting individual appointments, as with 'advice and consent of Senate' appointments in the United States. There is no legal basis for the second route in the Scotland Act, and its development in practice would depend on the Executive being willing, or required by political realities, to concede the right. It is clear that the British Government favours the first route, stating in the White Paper:

'The Scottish Executive will be required to put arrangements into place to ensure that appointments to public bodies are subject to independent scrutiny and conform to the Commissioner of Public Appointments' Code of Practice'. (8)

The Scotland Act appears to contain no provision for enforcing this requirement. Nevertheless, an early decision for the Executive and Parliament is whether to continue under the existing UK Code and Commissioner, or establish a separate Scottish one. Parliament would then have to determine its own mechanisms for scrutinising that process, for example through establishing a specialist Public Services Committee as in the UK House of Commons.

Scrutiny and accountability for activities

Both the Scotland Act and the CSG Report on the Scottish Parliament are silent on how Parliament might scrutinise the activities of Scottish public bodies, since this is implicitly seen as part of overall scrutiny of the Executive, rather than a special issue. The White Paper merely states:

'The Government wishes to leave detailed arrangements for the Scottish Parliament and its Executive to develop for themselves'.(9)

Subject committees of Parliament would be the obvious candidates for undertaking scrutiny, but may not be the best means of picking up overall issues, which might require a general Public Services Committee. Potential overlap with the work of the Audit Committee proposed by the CSG would also have to be considered. The experience of the UK House of Commons is that detailed scrutiny of the work of non-departmental bodies is uneven. One way of trying to avoid this would be to have a rolling programme of reviews over a period of years, though because the number of bodies in each subject area varies, this would imply an uneven workload.

There are five different types of body in which Parliament and its committees might take an interest:

Scottish bodies under the remit of the Parliament

These are the most straightforward, but it is worth noting:

(a) the potential costs for small bodies of extra Parliamentary accountability given existing levels of accountability to the Executive.

(b) potential UK interest, when even the most obscure Scottish agricultural research centre can generate findings of world-wide impact.

British bodies carrying out devolved functions

The White Paper (para. 2.10) makes it clear that the Scottish Parliament will have the power to require the submission of reports and the presentation of oral evidence and to investigate, report and debate on what they do. This raises the possibility that a body may be require to deal with up to four Parliaments or assemblies at once.

British coordinating bodies where there is a separate Scottish body

The example of the UK Sports Council has already been mentioned. The Parliament is most likely to be interested in the Scottish body operating in the area, but may wish occasionally to scrutinise directly or indirectly how the work of the coordinating body affects Scotland.

British bodies outside devolved functions, but with overlapping remits

Examples would be the research councils, which are not devolved, but clearly have an interest in general higher education funding. Another would be the Employment Service, which is not devolved, but might find it difficult to operate some of its schemes without the cooperation of the Enterprise network and other devolved bodies. There is to an extent a mutual interest between such bodies and the Scottish Executive and Parliament.

British bodies which are clearly in reserved areas but are important to Scotland

The White Paper lists examples of bodies in this and the previous category, ranging from the Commission for Racial Equality to the Post Office. The Scottish Parliament will be able to 'invite' reports and evidence from such bodies, but in the context where the Scottish Parliament has little to offer in exchange.

Patriation of GB/UK bodies

The one area relating to public bodies which is spelt out in some detail relates to British wide bodies operating in policy areas devolved to the Scottish Parliament and Executive. The White Paper states the British Government's view:

> 'The Government envisage however that the Scottish Parliament will want to continue most such UK or GB arrangements in the light of the advantages of sharing knowledge and expertise on a UK or GB basis and of the greater efficiency in the use of resources'. (10)

However, since it will be for the Scottish Executive and Parliament to arrive at their own judgement on this, the Scotland Act sets out in considerable detail in sections 88-90 the arrangements by which the activities and assets of the cross-border bodies would be divided.

Review of appropriateness of use of public bodies

Concern about appointments and scrutiny of existing activities is focused on the existing framework of public body activity. The Scottish Parliament could also choose to play a role in considering whether public bodies are the most appropriate form for these activities.

Among the questions are:

- Should government be involved in this activity at all?
- Would existing general local government be more appropriate?
- Would special purpose directly or indirectly elected local authorities be more appropriate?
- Should the activity be carried out directly by a department of the Executive, or an agency within one?

Conclusion

In its opening weeks the Scottish Parliament will be overwhelmed with issues to consider. Its role in relation to public bodies operating in Scotland could easily be overlooked. The relative silence of the Scotland Act and the CSG Report does not indicate a lack of issues to consider.

Chapter Thirteen:
The Role of Local Government

Mark McAteer and Michael Bennett

In legal and constitutional terms, when the Scottish Parliament inherits the powers currently in Westminster with respect to local government, little will change for local authorities. The devolution of power is in many ways a simple democratisation of the current powers and processes held by the Scottish Office. As one commentator noted:

> 'The legal nature of the relationship between local government in Scotland and the new [Scottish] Parliament and its Executive will be very similar to the current tripartite relationship involving local government, Parliament and the Secretary of State for Scotland.' (1).

In other words, local government will still be subject to central control. Local authorities will be highly dependent on and accountable to the Scottish Executive and their structures and functions will be determined by the Parliament and subject to control via the Scottish Office. Local spending limits will remain subject to tight central control and both the Executive and the Parliament will exercise a high degree of influence over key policy areas for local government. This is not surprising as the Scotland Act has transferred responsibility for all the functions and powers of local government in Scotland to the Parliament. Some of the responsibilities of local government that will be affected are outlined below in Table Fifteen.

Table Fifteen: Some Functions and Responsibilities of Local Government

Education
Local Planning
Social Work
Development Control
Police
Urban Development
Fire
Housing
Strategic Planning
Building Control
Roads and Road Safety
Libraries
Public Transport
Leisure and Recreation
Administration of Housing Benefit
Harbours
Archaeology
General Licensing
Coastal Protection
Listed Buildings and Ancient Monuments
Council Tax
Burial and Cremation
District Courts
Slaughterhouses
Ferries
Traffic Wardens
Food Hygiene, Standards and Labelling
Waste Collection and Disposal

While little in practical terms will change in the first instance the advent of the Parliament presents a unique opportunity to redefine the nature of central-local relations within Scotland. As an institution founded on the principle of subsidiarity the Parliament offers a real opportunity to challenge the centralisation of political power that we have witnessed in the United Kingdom over the last 20 years and accord local government an enhanced role in the governance of Scotland. However, the challenge of doing so is likely to be complicated by a wider context within which several crucial factors external to central-local relations will be of importance.

Redefining Central-Local Relations

An Independent Commission on Local Government and the Scottish Parliament, led by former Strathclyde Region Chief Executive Neil McIntosh, was established by the Government to report to the First Minister on ways that local government's legitimacy could be increased. (2) Its existence will be made more secure under the Parliament. While the Parliament will not be bound by the Commission's findings it will, in all likelihood play a key role in defining the shape and scope of the relationship. Some of the issues considered by the Commission are currently being discussed widely in local government circles and are at the core of future possible relations.

The simple fact that the Parliament will exist as a legislative body focused on governing Scotland means that the Executive, and committees, of the Parliament will have more time to introduce and enact legislation affecting Scotland. The Consultative Steering Group on the Scottish Parliament (CSG) anticipate anything from 10 to 12 pieces of primary legislation a year under the Parliament. (3) As a major public sector actor local government could be subject to new legislation on a more regular basis than it currently experiences under Westminster - where it has been one of the most heavily legislated areas over the last twenty years. A key issue is will this new legislative capacity engender a new form of centralisation within Scotland? Within local government circles there is a fear that the Parliament could become a 'super' council taking over where the previous regional councils left off and so undermining the current unitary local government system.

In order to offset this possibility the Commission, among others, has proposed the possibility of establishing a 'covenant' between local government, the Parliament and the Executive. The covenant would establish clear guidelines relating to central-local relations and by embracing the principle of subsidiarity it could secure the role of local government under the Parliament and could guarantee local government a role in the legislative processes of the Parliament (by defining it as a partner to be widely consulted in areas affecting its competencies). Alternatively local government could be given a more formal role in the pre-legislative process whereby it would play a role in developing possible legislative options for consideration in conjunction with the Executive or a Parliamentary committee. If such key roles are granted to local government it could become involved in scrutiny and other functions in partnership, with the Parliament, as it oversees the actions of the Executive. Thus the creation of the Parliament and the machinery of government that goes with it offers the possibility of ensuring that local and central governments interact and engage with one another in ways not feasible within current Westminster arrangements.

If however, we are to proceed in this manner some key issues will have to be clarified with respect to both the content of the covenant and how it is 'policed'. There is a danger that by enshrining central-local relations in a formal document any disputes over the interpretation of the covenant could lead to a legalistic process being embarked upon by either party to the covenant. This would undermine the principles of a covenant and notions of partnership embodied in it. To avoid this, a clear definition of the terms of the partnership would be required. While the partnership will not be one between equals it must be more than a simple rhetorical commitment to work together. It must ensure clarity with respect to the competencies of local and central government and ensure that partnership means more than just the right of local government to be consulted on relevant issues.

Some would like to see the covenant grant local authorities a power of general competence, which would allow it to pursue the interests of local citizens without the need for a legislative basis for its actions. In order to police the implementation of the covenant there may be merit in establishing a joint forum consisting of both Parliamentarians and local government representatives. Such a forum could produce an annual report on central-local relations in Scotland and act as a mediator if disputes arise between the Parliament and local government. Such a forum could provide added advantages by promoting greater contact between the two levels of government, which could lead to initiatives such as joint training for MSPs and councillors or even exchanges between both politicians and officials in local and central government.

If the covenant is to be of value, it must form the basis for greater levels of trust and respect between central and local government in Scotland. This will require central government to recognise local government as a democratically mandated institution that represents differentiation and localness from across Scotland. Equally local government must recognise the right of the Parliament to pursue the uniformity of social and political rights across Scotland, and to insist on an equal standard of service from the public sector for all Scottish citizens. Thus any attempt to define central and local relations in the form of a covenant is likely to be problematic as the two sides represent contradictory positions. That is not to say that a covenant will not be useful, but the document itself must merely be the embodiment of a greater willingness to strike an appropriate balance that secures control for what is rightly local at the local level and what is rightly national at the national level. However, in seeking such an agreement there are likely to be disputes and tensions and it is to some of those issues that we now turn.

Possible Tensions in Central-Local Relations

Many of the current well-publicised problems of Scottish local government arise from the highly centralised finance system which will continue to operate under the Parliament. The systems acts as follows:

- Total public expenditure, including local spending, is planned by central government, which specifies expenditure ceilings on local authority revenue expenditure, 'capping', and a ceiling on borrowing, 'borrowing consents'.

- Central government controls directly 84%-85% of local income through control of grant levels and the central determination, pooling and allocation of non-domestic rate income (NDRI).

- Consequently, a 1% increase in local spending above the level assumed by the grant and non-domestic rate income settlement requires an increase in council tax of 6%-7% - the so-called 'gearing' effect.

If the Scottish Parliament is to promote, and not merely express a commitment to, subsidiarity (4) then examining central controls on local income and expenditure is a precondition for this. The financing of local government clearly has to reflect its role and purpose as seen by society. If local government is to adopt a wider role, in particular the broad purpose of promoting community wellbeing, then changes to the legal framework (e.g. establishing a covenant) and changes to the financial framework are necessary. Specifically, the following issues may require priority attention in the post-devolution Scotland.

First, should local government spending continue to be planned for within the Scottish Parliament's block allocation from Westminster?

Under the devolution package local government spending will be calculated as part of the Parliament's block allocation from Westminster and it will account for around 40% of the Parliament's expenditure. Of more significance though is that the local authority self-financed element of spending (local taxation) will also be subject to control by the Parliament as the Westminster Treasury regard it as an indirect source of taxation. The Treasury with its desire for 100% public budget control argues that both are necessary.

The effect of current levels of central control is to negate the political decentralisation implicit within devolution and to minimise the scope for genuine local governance. The political rationale for local government, that it reflects local pluralism, diversity, and the different aspirations of different communities, appears to be rejected by these processes. The core point is that a judgement of priority will have to be explicitly made between central control of expenditure and local democracy. If it is not clarified it creates a position of almost complete non-accountability in the governance of Scotland despite the Parliament's supposed promotion of greater accountability. Both local councillors and Parliamentarians may 'blame' one another for the financial problems local authorities face - the councillor argues that they have no money as a consequence of central control while the Parliament will point to the level of local government spending as proof of its commitment. Both will, of course, be partially correct but the effect is that nobody is ultimately responsible for the state of local services.

Moreover, the future of the Scottish Block in a post-devolution UK will also be of critical importance. If, as some have suggested the Scottish Block will come under pressure in future years (see Chapter Nine) it is possible that local finance will be targeted to protect the Parliament's financial position. Without doubt local finance could not escape scrutiny if Scottish public finance is under severe pressure at the UK level. However, any examination of local finance in such a scenario would have to be conducted in the light of those issues being argued over at the UK level - namely social need criteria. If Scottish public spending is to be defended in social need terms at the UK level equal consideration must be given to the social need impact of reductions in local financial discretion and expenditure within Scotland. It would be anomalous if the Parliament argued that social need justifies Scottish public expenditure within the UK and then ignored it at the local level to protect the Parliament's finances. Such a scenario may also lead to a re-examination of the distribution processes within the Scottish local government finance system to ensure social need criteria are given a more prominent role than currently prevails.

Lastly, the system of Capital Consents to local authorities - that is permission to borrow - also negates local choice and could cause tensions. The Comprehensive Spending Review (CSR) has relaxed Treasury thinking on borrowing matters to some degree - the Government now distinguishes between public borrowing for revenue deficit purposes and for investment purposes - but overall control of local borrowing by the centre remains. The Parliament's ability to control investment across the public sector will be of major importance and a necessary part of its ability to promote economic and social wellbeing within Scotland. However, if Treasury control over local public borrowing continues, despite being small in the overall context of public investment, then a key area of conflict could erupt and impact on central-local relations within Scotland. The issues in theory and practice here are complex, but important enough to warrant a detailed review of the theoretical and policy arguments for control and the Scottish Parliament, working in partnership with local government should promote this.

A further possible tension point could emerge around an attempt to build genuinely holistic public services in Scotland as envisaged in the government's community planning agenda. Although still at a pilot stage, 'Community Planning' will oblige local authorities and their partners in the public and private sectors to formalise joint-working procedures to deliver services around common purposes. However, it is difficult to see how services and issues such as community care, education and social inclusion can be adequately developed without partnership between the appropriate public and private agencies. If however, local actors fail to pursue this to any real depth there is a real danger that the Parliament will proceed to co-ordinate matters better and take control to ensure a genuine holistic approach to public services across Scotland.

Until the political composition of the Parliament is known, it is difficult to predict with any certainty its dynamics and impact on local government. However, there is a real opportunity to revisit old arguments and resolve old disputes. But without a genuine partnership to pursue these matters that opportunity may be lost and Scotland will remain locked within a cycle of conflict between central and local government. We are not arguing that the Scottish

Parliament should have no controls over local government or no control over revenues allocated to local government in the form of grants, but a change in central-local relations is desirable to eliminate the centralist bias of the present system, and the capacity, whether used or not, that it generates for central control.

Chapter Fourteen:
Relations with Westminster Michelle Mitchell

The establishment of the Scottish Parliament changes the face of Scottish politics forever. However, we do not have to wait until the summer 1999 to witness devolution. In many ways power has already shifted from Westminster to Edinburgh. No major Scottish legislation was included in this year's (1998/99) Queen's Speech. It is accepted that it would be inappropriate for Westminster to legislate on matters solely affecting Scotland. Scottish Office Ministers are spending more and more time away from Westminster. They know only too well that the future of their political careers depends on their getting seats in the Holyrood Parliament. No wonder Scots are increasingly asking, 'Westminster? Where?' Or more aptly, 'Westminster? Why?'

However, it should not be assumed that Scottish devolution is a dead issue at Westminster. On the contrary, Parliament is just waking up to the fact that life at Westminster is going to be fundamentally altered as a direct consequence of devolving power to Scotland. It is not just a matter for the Scots. Devolution raises fundamental questions about the nature of government in the UK. The Scottish Affairs Select Committee has published a report on Multi-Layer Democracy which examined the devolution settlement (1) and the Procedure Select Committee has just set up an inquiry into the consequences of devolution. (2)

Some changes are already known, and their starkest effect will be in the ministerial make-up of the Scottish Office. With responsibility for matters such as health, education and law and order being transferred to Edinburgh on July 1st 1999, a ministerial reshuffle may reduce the number of Scottish Ministers from seven to a likely two. Before long, only the Secretary of State will remain, and even this post is not guaranteed, as a Cabinet post may no longer be justifiable when the rump of the Secretary of State's work is reduced to negotiating the annual block grant and managing the relationship with the Scottish Parliament, but in the short term change will be kept to a minimum. In time, the two posts of Secretary of State for Scotland and Wales might combine in a single Secretary of State for Territorial Affairs, who could be attached to the Cabinet Office.

Answering the West Lothian Question

The number of Scottish seats at Westminster will be reduced from 72 seats to approximately 57 seats. The Scotland Act 1998 (Section 86) repeals Scotland's protected minimum of 71 seats. The next Parliamentary Boundary Commission Review, due to be completed 2004/2005 is likely to recommend a 15-seat reduction, thus ending Scotland's over-representation at Westminster. These recommendations will come into effect sometime after the 2002 General Election.

In the meantime, what will Scottish MPs do at Westminster? Most of their constituents will look to the Scottish Parliament to address their grievances, since it is they who will making decisions on issues that affect people's everyday lives. However, being an effective MP is not just about answering constituency queries, important as this is. The prime functions of the House of Commons are to scrutinise the Executive and hold it to account. Parliament does not always perform these functions effectively. MPs need to be given a meaningful, defined role in Parliament. Scottish devolution puts pressure on Westminster to change its own procedures. Reform of the Commons has been very slow so far, and the Modernisation Committee has achieved little tangible reform. Devolution may provide much-needed impetus for modernising the Commons.

Pressure is already mounting for the Prime Minister to ban Scottish MPs serving as Ministers in departments dealing with England and Wales. Some English MPs want to reduce the influence of their Scottish colleagues over English legislation: The West Lothian Question (see Chapter Twenty for more information). Scots will be increasingly viewed as interfering in exclusively English affairs. It is feared by some, that the constantly predicted English backlash would quickly become a reality.

One way of avoiding this would be to curtail the voting rights of Scottish, Welsh and Northern Irish MPs at Westminster, by disqualifying them from intervening and voting in debates on English legislation post-devolution. However, the Government is likely to resist changes of this kind, fearing the emergence of two-classes of MPs, and instead, favours re-establishing the Standing Committee on Regional Affairs. Rt. Hon Margaret Beckett MP announced in Business Questions on January 14th 1999:

'I hope in the very near future, to put some proposals before the Modernisation Committee on the use of procedures of the House that allow for a Standing Committee on the English regions... It will be an exclusively English forum where English MPs will meet to discuss exclusively English affairs - it will take the form of an English Grand Committee'. (6)

A Standing Committee on Regional Affairs already exists under standing order 117. It consists of all members for English constituencies, with up to five others, and last met on July 26th 1978. Between 1975-8 it met regularly and provided a forum for members to raise issues of concern about their respective regions.

The English Grand Committee could follow the precedent of the Scottish and Welsh Grand Committees. The committees had no legislative function and were widely criticised in Scotland and Wales as 'toothless talking shops' and a 'very poor substitute for real devolution'. Now the Scottish Parliament is to be established, there is no reason why an English Grand Committee should not assume more of the legislative powers of a devolved assembly.

Scottish Business at Westminster

In the light of Scottish devolution, the Speaker will need to develop a new set of rules defining those devolved matters on which debate will be no longer allowed at Westminster. The best precedent is Stormont, in Northern Ireland. Issues that have been delegated to Scottish Parliament must be raised in that body. On reserved matters, such as abortion and broadcasting, the appropriate Minister in Whitehall will continue to be questioned.

Changes may occur in the amount of time allocated to Scottish matters at Westminster after the Holyrood Parliament is set up. At the moment Scottish MPs have 40 minutes once a month to question Scottish ministers on the floor of the Commons concerning their area of responsibility. After May 1999, virtually all those matters will become the responsibility of the new Parliament in Edinburgh, and consequently, Scottish Question Time will be abolished.

The future of the Scottish Grand Committee is also under threat. All Scottish MPs are members of the Scottish Grand Committee, which has traditionally been a forum to debate issues of concern chosen by the opposition. Post-devolution, it is difficult to see what role a Scottish Grand Committee would play at Westminster. The future of the Scottish. Affairs Committee is also doubtful. It scrutinises the work of the Scottish Office Standing Committee, established ad-hoc for the Committee stage of Scottish Bills. It is likely that the Procedure Committee will take evidence from the chairs of the Scottish Grand Committee and Scottish Affairs committee on how they see their roles post devolution. The Scottish Affairs Select Committee recommended that the House amend its Standing Orders, so that it could carry out inquiries into the work of all Departments of State insofar as it affects Scotland. It also saw a role for the committee in assisting communications between the two Parliaments.

Westminster will continue to pass legislation affecting Scotland and even on devolved matters (Scotland Act, Sections 28 and 29). Generally it will do so by consent, for example to comply with international obligations, but this may occasionally be forced, as happened in the history of the Stormont Parliament. (7)

Intergovernmental Relations

The Scotland Act 1998 lays down the division of powers between London and Scotland but says very little about their continuing relations will be managed. Donald Dewar describes how intergovernmental relations will work:

> 'They will be based on consultation, consent and co-operation at official and ministerial level, buttressed where necessary by non-statutory agreements between Departments. No provision is required or made in the Scotland Bill, because relations will evolve and build on good working relationships between Whitehall and the Scottish Office.' (8)

There will be a significant degree of overlap between the Scottish Parliament and Westminster. Drafts of concordats between Whitehall and the Scottish Parliament recognise this. A concordat is a non-statutory agreement, which is not subject to approval by Westminster or the Scottish Parliament.

They are likely to be signed between civil services and officials rather than Ministers, except on specific occasions and set down common processes and main features of good working relations, rather than specifying substantive outcomes.

The Scottish Parliament is unlikely to play much of a role in determining inter-governmental relations. The Scottish Executive and British Executive will work together in this area, as is reflected in the establishment of the Joint Ministerial Committee (JMC). The Government recognised during the final stages of the Scotland Bill that there was a lack of institutions to ensure effective liaison and the resolution of disputes between the centre and the periphery. The JMC, administered through the Cabinet Office, will be the forum where key relationships are worked through, where grievances are dealt with, and disputes resolved. Key members of the Scottish, Northern Irish, Welsh and UK Executives will regularly attend, and it will allow the UK administration to engage at the highest level with the leadership of the devolved Assemblies in a situation where there is no shared collective responsibility.

Quite independently from the processes of devolution in Scotland and Wales, the British-Irish Council arising from the Belfast Agreement could be influential in shaping the course of devolution. The British-Irish Council involves the UK and Republic of Ireland governments and representatives from the Scottish, Welsh and Northern Ireland Assemblies, the Channel Islands and the Isle of Man. The Council will discuss issues of concern to both Britain and Ireland without having any specific responsibility. It is a ready-made institution, which will allow Wales, Scotland and Northern Ireland jointly to negotiate positions prior to the meeting of the Joint Ministerial Committee.

Reform of the House of Lords also provides an excellent opportunity to improve inter-governmental relations. A reformed House of Lords could integrate the different parts of the UK into a central institution.The Second Chamber could represent these interests and act as a Chamber of the Union. (9)

Cornes has suggested that inter-governmental conferences could be improved by holding Summit Meetings, similar to those held in Europe, with the main political figures in the Executive bodies of the devolved institutions and Westminster. Ministerial committee meetings could take place in specific policy areas such as education. Meetings between civil servants in relevant policy areas could parallel these. (10) Meetings with officials are likely to form the main place where most of the work is done. Intergovernmental structures will be crucial in ensuring good relations between Westminster and the Scottish Parliament.

However, there will be times when conflict does arise. How disputes are resolved is crucial in the relationship between the London and Edinburgh political systems under devolution. We should be under no illusion that the dispute mechanism will be tested, and should expect friction between Westminster and Edinburgh as the Parliament begins to flex its political muscles and test its legislative boundaries. The scope and extent of the Scottish Parliament's legislative competence is defined in a number of the Bill's provisions. The Parliament has the power to make laws only on areas that have been devolved, and an Act of the Scottish Parliament which touches on matters reserved to Westminster will be formally invalid. This will not stop a Scottish Executive from deliberately trespassing into areas that are formally reserved. The dispute process could be used to score political points, for example, questioning the legitimacy of broadcasting as a reserved matter. Of course there will be times when the Scottish and UK Governments will have different views on the Scottish Parliament's legislative competence particularly over finance and funding, the position of the UK Government is taking in international negotiations (including the EU), and the right to secede.

A number of mechanisms are outlined in the Scotland Act to ensure that legislation passed by the Scottish Parliament does not exceed its remit:

1. The Scottish Executive has to certify that Bills will be within legislative competence of the Scottish Parliament (Section 31). This must be done before a Bill is introduced, or at the time of its introduction.

2. Standing Orders will ensure that a Bill cannot be introduced into the Parliament if the Presiding Office decides that it or any of its provisions are outside the Parliament's competence. However, Standing Orders may provide for the Presiding Officer to be overruled, and for the Bill not to be submitted for Royal Assent until a reference has been made to the Judicial Committee of the Privy Council under Clause 32 or 33. The Bill cannot receive Royal Assent if the Judicial Committee has decided that it is not within the Parliament's legislative competence (Section 32).

3. The Advocate General, the Lord Advocate, or the Attorney General may refer the question of whether a Bill or any of its provisions is within the legislative competence of the Scottish Parliament to the Judicial Committee. Under Section 33, four

weeks is stipulated after the passing of the Bill but before Royal Assent.

4. The Scottish Secretary of State may intervene under Section 35 if he has 'reasonable grounds' to believe that a Bill would be incompatible with international obligations. Or if a Bill 'would have an adverse effect on the operation of an enactment as it applies in relation to reserved matters'.

5. A Bill may be reconsidered if the Judicial Committee decides that it is not within the Parliament's legislative competence, or if an order is made by the Secretary of State under Section 35. There is no equivalent therefore to the broad powers given to the Secretary of State in the Scotland Act 1978 to recommend that a Scottish Bill be struck down on the grounds that it might affect a reserved power, and its enactment would not be in the public interest.

6. There is a provision for a review after Royal Assent under Section 98 and Schedule 6. The Privy Council is the final court of appeal for devolution issues. This includes the question of whether an Act of the Scottish Parliament is within its legislative competence and is defined in para 1 of Schedule 6.

Not all cases will go to the Privy Council but even a small increase in its workload could be difficult to manage, particularly if they are big cases requiring urgent solution. Also, there is a split at the apex of the judicial structure, with the House of Lords remaining as the highest court of appeal and the Privy Council as the highest court in relation to devolution matters. There will be occasions when devolution and other law matters intermingle, which could result in a lack of coherence in case law. The European Court of Justice may also influence the nature of the devolution settlement.

So Scottish devolution is on the way, but its consequences are by no means clear. Devolution is not just a Scottish development but one with profound consequences for the UK. (11) We should expect a series of changes at Westminster and possible tensions between the United Kingdom and Scottish Parliaments in the next few years.

Chapter Fifteen:
Relations with the European Union

Noreen Burrows

The UK joined the European Economic Community (now known more generally as the European Union or EU) in 1973. Membership gives certain rights to Member States and imposes obligations on them. Perhaps the most important right is to participate in the work of the European institutions where policy is formulated and legally binding rules are agreed. Undoubtedly the most important obligation is to obey these rules once they have been agreed.

The three most important political institutions are:

- The European Parliament is made up of MEPs elected from the 15 Member States of the EU, 8 of whom are from Scotland.

- The European Commission made up of 20 Commissioners, nominated by the Member States but independent of them and having the power to initiate European legislation.

- The Council of Ministers made up of one minister from each Member State with a changing membership depending on the subject matter e.g. agriculture with Ministers of Agriculture, finance with Ministers of Finance.

The European Parliament and the Council of Ministers jointly adopt legislation in some areas, while in others the Council adopts legislation after consulting the Parliament. Once rules are adopted in Brussels they generally have to be implemented and enforced in the Member States.

The European institutions are supported by a complex web of committees and working groups, some made up of national experts or civil servants seconded from Member States. The Council of Ministers is supported by a Committee of Permanent Representatives (COREPER) made up of senior national civil servants based in Brussels supported by officials seconded from the civil service. They liase with other European representatives and with government departments at home. This level of representation is known as UKREP. There is also a Committee of the Regions bringing together representatives of local authorities and regional governments and Scotland has four representatives here, all from local government. An Economic and

Social Council represents consumers, business and trade unions.

Relations with the EU are therefore complex, and devolution adds a further level. EU matters are reserved, except for the implementation and enforcement of European rules which is devolved. However, many powers devolved to the Scottish Parliament are also ones where European policies and rules already apply. Agriculture is devolved but the European Common Agricultural policy limits what a Scottish Parliament could do. The Scottish Parliament and the Scottish Executive need to be involved, therefore, in European affairs.

The Scottish Parliament and Executive have responsibility for ensuring that European rules are applied effectively in Scotland. The Scotland Act specifically states that any action by the Parliament or the Executive that breaches a European rule is ultra vires (outside their powers). The Westminster Parliament and the Secretary of State for Scotland can intervene to prevent any breach of a European law by the devolved institutions. The Judicial Committee of the Privy Council, the court responsible for dealing with devolution issues, can strike down any Act of the Scottish Parliament that breaches European law. Westminster can also legislate on European matters for Scotland even in devolved areas and UK Ministers retain the power to make delegated legislation implementing European rules for Scotland. These powers are necessary because it is the UK that is the Member State of the EU, and the UK could be brought before the European Court for any breach of European law by any of the devolved administrations.

European aspects of policy will therefore be raised at three different levels of government - in Edinburgh, London and Brussels. Co-ordination and co-operation will be required between these levels to ensure consistency in approach and to minimise confrontation over European matters. The Scottish Affairs Select Committee recognised this when it stated that:

> 'No-where is the reliance of the whole devolution package on compromise, goodwill and reasonableness so apparent as in respect of relations with the EU'. (1)

European matters within the Scottish Parliament

The Scottish Parliament needs access to information about proposed policy developments to be taken at the European level so that it can feed into the policy making process where the interests of Scotland are particularly affected. It will need to take a view on policy proposals and put these views, as appropriate, to the Scottish Ministers, to the UK government and to the European institutions. It will also need to ensure that European law is observed in Scotland. Parliament has several options on how to deal with European matters, and some are listed below.

European Committee

The Consultative Steering Group (CSG) has proposed that one committee of the new Parliament should be a European Committee. Its proposed remit is:

- to sift relevant EU related documents on behalf of the Parliament - bearing in mind the several hundreds of documents published by the EU each year.

- to take further action as necessary either within the committee or by referring the matter to another committee or to the plenary.

- to debate wider EU issues.

The Committee is likely to be made up of members from other committees. For example, if there is to be a committee on agriculture then a representative will sit on the European Committee since there is a significant European dimension to agriculture. The convener of the European Committee is not likely to sit on any other committee since the volume of work will be enormous. Some discussion has taken place on whether the membership of the Committee might be expanded by co-option of other individuals with expertise in European matters. MEPs, for example, might assist the committee in its deliberations.

It would be impossible for the European Committee to attempt to deal with all matters coming from Brussels. It needs to set priorities for Scotland and concentrate on these. It will have a role to play in scrutinising proposed legislation and analysing how proposed legislation would affect Scottish interests and existing law and policies. It could also have a proactive role by proposing policy developments that could then be forwarded either to the Scottish Ministers or to the UK government or to the European Commission or Parliament. The committee could also question Scottish Ministers on European matters or conduct enquiries.

It would also be useful if the European Committee of the Scottish

Parliament could co-operate with the various European Committees in Westminster. This would in the first instance have to be an informal arrangement as there are no existing mechanisms for inter-parliamentary co-ordination. The advantage of such co-operation is that the UK government has accepted a so-called 'Parliamentary scrutiny reserve' which is an undertaking not to commit the UK in the Council of Ministers until parliamentary scrutiny is completed unless national interests would be adversely affected. This undertaking operates in relation to Westminster but not, at the moment, to the Scottish Parliament so co-operation between the Scottish and UK parliaments on European matters would seem sensible.

Representation in Brussels

It has been reported that some Scottish Office officials are in favour of opening a European Office of the Scottish Executive in Brussels, to act as an intelligence gatherer and a visible sign of Scottish interests in Brussels. It has been suggested that the new office would share premises with Scotland Europa, set up several years ago to represent the views of Scottish business, local authorities and other Scottish-based organisations such as universities. There is also the possibility that the Scottish Parliament could open a Brussels office. Another proposal is that the new Scottish Administration might second representatives to work in UKREP to co-ordinate the UK position and to represent Scottish Ministers. (It is interesting to note that the European Parliament appointed a spokesperson in Edinburgh in early 1999).

Membership of CLARE

CLARE is the Conference of Legislative Regional Assemblies set up in 1997, which holds regular meetings between the President of the European Parliament and its equivalents in regional parliaments (the Presiding Officer in Scotland). It is a way of giving regional parliaments access to documents from the European Parliament via electronic databases and a means of networking at the regional level. Representatives of CLARE can also attend meetings of the European Parliament's Regional Affairs Committee to try to develop a two-way flow of information. It is reported that the Scottish Parliament has been invited to participate in the work of CLARE but this is for the Parliament to decide after the elections.

Committee of the Regions

Scotland has four representatives (and four alternates) on the Committee of the Regions. In the UK these representatives have come from local government but in other countries where there is a regional tier of government representation is usually divided between regional and local government. New representatives for CoR will be chosen in 2002 and it is likely that two members will be chosen from the Scottish Parliament and two from Scottish local authorities. Co-operation between the new Parliament and Scottish local government will be particularly important on European matters since there is existing overlap. The use of European funds in regional development, food safety and environment, for example, cross the boundary between European, Scottish and local government functions. It might be possible for the members of the CoR to assist the European Committee of the Scottish Parliament in their work.

The Scottish Ministers and Europe

European law dictates that any Minister who attends a Council of Ministers meeting in Brussels has the power to agree to decisions for the whole of his/her country. As the UK is the Member State of the EU, the Minister must be able to bind the whole of the UK. Scottish Ministers do not have this power since they operate in a purely Scottish context, and cannot, therefore, represent England, Wales or Northern Ireland. At the same time, they must be involved in the European policy-making process since much of what they do and the kind of legislation that they will need to introduce into Parliament, will be influenced by the EU. The White Paper on the Scottish Parliament stated that it is the UK Government's intention to involve Scottish Ministers and officials in developing UK policy towards Europe and where relevant, Scottish Ministers will have a role to play in Council meetings. Their role will be 'to support and advance the single negotiating line'. UK Ministers will lead the delegation as required by European rules but Scottish Ministers might speak on behalf of the UK where a Scottish Minister is part of the UK negotiating team.

These commitments in the White Paper were not translated into any formal consultation mechanism in the Scotland Act. What is now being discussed is the creation of semi-formal inter-ministerial mechanisms where European policy can be discussed and co-ordinated. Until the Scottish Ministers are appointed no agreements can be reached with the UK Government but three possibilities are currently being discussed:

- A joint ministerial committee
- An overarching Concordat on European Affairs
- British-Irish Council

Joint Ministerial Committee

The Joint Ministerial Committee (see Chapter Seven) will be able to discuss a wide range of matters of common interest to the UK government and the devolved administrations, and European policy is one area where such discussions will be crucial. The Select Committee on Scottish Affairs believes that this committee may have difficulties in agreeing on European matters. It stated that:

'There is considerable and legitimate potential scope for disagreement between states and sub-state (and even between sub-states) even where both administrations are of the same political complexion, but any disagreements will be exacerbated when they are not. And inevitably, even if the political control in the UK and in Scotland start off the same there will come a time when they differ . . . this makes the possibility of reaching common ground for a delegation to Brussels . . . more difficult to achieve'. (2)

An example shows how problematic this might become. If Scotland had a pro-European administration, and the UK a Euro-sceptic one, it is difficult to see what accommodation there might be between them on a joint European policy. If the Committee is established it might need to set out its working procedures ahead of such potential difficulties.

European Concordat

The proposed European Concordat is intended to cover how European policy will be discussed within and between government departments. According to the CSG report on the handling of European business the Concordat is intended to cover:

- arrangements for the timely exchange of information and policy proposals so that a single UK line can be agreed within the timetable determined by Brussels.
- attendance and participation by Scottish Ministers at EU Councils.

- arrangements for resolving disagreements, bearing in mind the need for a single UK line and to take the views of devolved administrations into account.

- implementation of EU obligations.

- handling of infraction proceedings where there is a failure to implement European law properly.

The scope and content of the Concordat are still being developed and agreement can only finally be reached after the elections.

British-Irish Council

The British-Irish Council is discussed more fully in Chapter Eighteen below. From the point of view of European policy it is important that one of the areas deemed suitable for early discussion in the BIC is how EU matters are to be approached. This suggests that there may be the possibility of a broader co-ordination of policy to include Ireland as well. In some areas this is more important than others. For example, both the UK and Ireland have opted out of some of the arrangements relating to free movement of persons under the Schengen arrangements that form part of the new Treaty of Amsterdam. This is because a common passport area exists between the UK and Ireland and both countries wish to retain these arrangements. However, both wish to be associated with some aspects of Schengen although the exact scope is still to be determined. Agriculture and farming may be another useful area for discussion. The BSE crisis was a problem crossing devolved, UK and Irish, and European responsibilities. Until the BIC is established it is too early to predict its success in co-ordinating European policies.

Chapter Sixteen:
The Role of Civil Society

Stephen Maxwell

The Westminster Parliament developed the principle of Parliamentary sovereignty which kept the public at a respectful distance from the processes of legislation and scrutiny of government. If the Members of the Scottish Parliament remain true to their parties' promises and the expectations of the Scottish public, the Scottish Parliament by contrast will engage Scottish society in an active and wide ranging collaboration in legislating and in scrutinising the Executive.

This commitment to engage with wider Scottish society comes partly from an ambition to establish the democratic credentials of the new Parliament and partly from a changed understanding of the requirements of effective government. In a complex modern society the state cannot govern by legislative fiat. It needs to inform and improve its policies by tapping the expertise and experience of society as a whole. And to implement its policies it needs to mobilise the support of organised social interests and groups outwith the state.

These interests and groups make up 'civil society'. In addition to being independent from the state, they are usually voluntary associations and are non-profit making. They range from trade unions and churches with hundreds of thousands of members, through political parties and professional and business associations, to small community-based organisations with a handful of supporters. The essence of their status as civil organisations is that they are set up by, and are accountable to, their own members, not to the state.

The Scottish Parliament's relationship with Scottish civil society will be influenced by the part civil organisations played in the genesis of the Parliament. In 1988 some of Scotland's leading civil organisations, including major Scottish Churches, the Scottish Trades Union Congress (STUC), and the Convention of Scottish Local Authorities (COSLA), formed the Scottish Constitutional Convention to develop and promote proposals for a Scottish Parliament. While the Parliament's status and powers differ in some important respects from the Convention's proposals, the Convention played a crucial part in keeping the issue of the Parliament near the top of the political agenda and informing public debate. Two members of the Convention's Steering Group were also members of the Consultative Steering Group (CSG) set up in January 1998 by the Scottish Office to develop proposals for procedures and Standing Orders of the Scottish Parliament, effectively the framework for Parliament's engagement with Scottish civil society.

There are two models for a Parliament's relationship with civil society, 'corporatist' and 'open'. In the corporatist model, certain organised interests are identified by the state as 'social partners' and given a guaranteed role in decision-taking, usually in an advisory capacity. This model is favoured by the European Union which gives trade union, business and consumer interests representation on consultative bodies such as the Economic and Social Committee. While the European Union's policy making and decision taking bodies are open to representations from other civil organisations the 'social partners' enjoy an institutional advantage in putting their views to the EU's policy makers.

In the open model the state makes no formal distinction between citizens and civil organisations, concentrating instead on making its decision-making processes as open as possible to all citizens, whether or not they are organised in groups.

The CSG's proposals largely reflect the open model. They recommend a range of measures to make the Scottish Parliament accessible to the Scottish public, including pre-legislative hearings on proposals for legislation, the use of IT, the appointment of individuals who are not members of Parliament as non-voting members of Parliamentary Committees, and formal rights of public petition. But they give a nod in the direction of the corporatist model by endorsing proposals for the creation of a Scottish Civic Forum through which the Scottish Trades Union Congress (STUC), the Confederation of British Industry (Scotland) (CBI Scotland), the Scottish Council for Voluntary Organisations (SCVO) and Action Together by Churches in Scotland (ACTS) would act as facilitators and guarantors of access to Parliament by civil organisations, particularly groups traditionally excluded from the decision-making process. While the CSG agrees that the Civic Forum must be created by, and accountable to, civil organisations, it suggests that it might receive some funding from Parliament.

How well equipped is Scottish civil society to act as a partner with the Scottish Parliament in policy making in the way envisaged by the

CSG and the advocates of a Scottish Civic Forum?

It has some obvious strengths. The Scottish Churches with a combined membership of 1.8m have a strong tradition as independent and forceful contributors to Scottish public debates. In the absence of a Scottish Parliament, the Church of Scotland's General Assembly earned in some quarters the honorary title 'Scotland's Parliament' for the range and seriousness of its debates on the Church and Nation Committee's annual deliverances on public issues. For long influential within the Labour Party the Catholic Church under the leadership of Cardinal Thomas Winning, has begun to speak out more publicly on a wide range of issues. While their corporate voice is less well known, both the Scottish Episcopal and the smaller Protestant churches have always had individuals willing and able to make effective interventions.

Even as the strength of its trade union membership base has diminished, the STUC has continued to play an important role in public debate including support for the Scottish Constitutional Convention. Individual trade unions, notably the public sector unions UNISON and TGWU, contribute vigorously to a wide range of public service, local government and social policy issues. While business associations have traditionally concentrated on 'behind the scenes' lobbying, the prospect of the Scottish Parliament with significant economic powers has stimulated established bodies such as CBI (Scotland), the Scottish Federation of Small Businesses and the Chambers of Commerce to play a more public role, and has given birth to new business groupings with links to political parties.

Like the business associations, the National Farmers' Union (Scotland) has often chosen to make representations behind the scenes though growing concern over farming's impact on the environment and the economic difficulties faced by farmers in recent years have forced the Union to seek a higher public profile.

Scotland also has a well developed range of professional associations. Although not autonomous bodies, the British Medical Association in Scotland and the Scottish Board of the Royal College of Nursing are frequent contributors on health policy issues. Other health organisations such as the Colleges of Surgeons and Physicians of Edinburgh and Glasgow and the Institute of Health Service Managers in Scotland are more often active behind the scenes.

The legal profession is even better entrenched in the shape of the Law Society of Scotland, the Bar Association of Glasgow and the Faculty of Advocates. Although part of the Scottish Office, the Scottish Law Commission makes an important expert contribution on the legal dimensions of policy issues.

The interests of teachers have a powerful voice in the Educational Institute of Scotland (EIS) and other smaller teachers' associations. By comparison the interests of higher and further education seem underrepresented in public debates despite the efforts of the Committee of Scottish Higher Education Principals and the Association of Scottish Colleges.

Social care interests also have a weak public presence. Neither the Association of Directors of Social Work nor the British Association of Social Workers (Scotland) have a public profile or influence corresponding to their responsibility for £1bn worth of services for hundreds of thousands of Scots in need of care or support.

While all agencies of civil society are technically voluntary associations, an important distinction is made between associations formed to promote a sectional, professional or religious interest, and organisations formed for public benefit. An estimated 40,000 such voluntary organisations exist in Scotland, about half of which are recognised as charities with associated tax privileges. The relationship which Parliament develops with this sector will provide the most severe test of its engagement with the full diversity of Scottish society.

Scotland's voluntary organisations range from major providers of publicly funded services with incomes of several million pounds to small locally based groups with a handful of members and perhaps just a few pounds in a bank account. They represent both a great reservoir of experience in the policy areas controlled by the Scottish Parliament and an extensive, albeit complex, structure for two-way communication between Parliament and society.

A small minority of voluntary organisations will have the political and financial resources to represent their own views to Parliament, through paid policy or Parliamentary officers. Organisations in particular policy areas, for example, the environment, disability, and housing, already have standing forums or policy networks to represent their collective interests to policy makers. The Parliament will stimulate the creation of other networks representing broad voluntary sector interests. Smaller organisations will find it more difficult to access Parliament directly. Some will hope to use the opportunities provided by the Parliament's IT channels. Others may look to dedicated advice and information services provided by the Parliament itself or by independent bodies such as the Scottish Council for Voluntary Organisations, the umbrella body for the sector.

The vigour of Scottish civil society will depend critically on the intellectual resources on which it can call. While the four older Scottish universities have been criticised in the recent past for failing to apply their intellectual skills to Scottish issues, Scotland's other universities, old and new, are now steadily expanding their contribution to research and policy development with a Scottish focus.

One area where Scottish civil society is under-equipped is in the independent policy think tanks which from a mainly London base play so influential a part in policy development at the United Kingdom level. However, in the last decade a number of new public policy institutes have been launched, including the Centre for Scottish Public Policy and the Scottish Council Foundation. The style of open participative government expected to be adopted by the Parliament will require a further substantial increase in the contribution of independent policy expertise, whether from universities and colleges, voluntary organisations or dedicated policy institutes to broaden the work and networks of the Scottish policy communities, academics, intellectuals and all those interested in the future of public policy in Scotland.

Chapter Seventeen:
The Equality Agenda

Morag Alexander and Joan Stringer

How far do the powers and responsibilities of the Scottish Parliament match the equality agenda set by the Scottish Constitutional Convention? The Convention Report outlines the agenda as:

- the Scottish Parliament should have power under Scots Law to combat discrimination 'in whatever form it arises';

- the Scottish Parliament should be able to promote equal opportunities 'for women, people with disabilities, ethnic minority communities and other groups';

- the membership of the Parliament should be gender balanced. (1)

Under the terms of the Scotland Act, the Scottish Parliament will not be responsible for the Equal Pay Act (1970), the Sex Discrimination Act (1975), the Race Relations Act (1976) and the Disability Discrimination Act (1995), nor for the statutory bodies charged with law enforcement and promotion under these Acts, the Equal Opportunities Commission (EOC), the Commission for Racial Equality (CRE) and the National Disability Council (NDC). This means that all discrimination laws, their operation and review will continue to be the responsibility of Westminster. So women and men who wish to claim their rights under the sex, race and disability discrimination laws will continue to be governed by Westminster legislation, not by legislation of the Scottish Parliament and Scots Law, as proposed by the Scottish Constitutional Convention. It also means that the sponsoring Departments for the statutory bodies will remain as at present: the Department for Education and Employment (for the EOC); the Home Office (for the CRE); the Department for Education and Employment (for the NDC).

However, the Scottish Parliament will not be able to pass legislation which is in breach of European Community law or the European Convention on Human Rights (2) and therefore will be directly bound by European sex equality laws including Article 119 of the Treaty of Rome, the Equal Treatment and the Equal Pay Directives.

While the Scottish Parliament will not be responsible for equality legislation, the Scotland Act details exceptions to this general reservation of the discrimination laws to Westminster. (3) These exceptions give the Scottish Parliament the power to:

- encourage equal opportunities and in particular to secure the observance of the requirements of the law relating to equal opportunities;

- ensure that Scottish public authorities do not discriminate;

- ensure that cross-border public authorities do not discriminate in their Scottish functions.

The Scotland Act defines those entitled to 'equal opportunities' more broadly than the current Westminster legislation, which covers only sex, race and disability:

'Equal opportunities means the prevention, elimination or regulation of discrimination between persons on grounds of sex or marital status, on racial grounds, or on grounds of disability, age, sexual orientation, language or social origin, or of other personal attributes, including beliefs or opinions, such as religious beliefs or political opinions'. (4)

Referring back to the agenda set by the Scottish Constitutional Convention, while the Scottish Parliament will have no power to enforce discrimination legislation, it will have the power to promote equal opportunities to a wider range of people than currently covered by Westminster legislation.

The Consultative Steering Group (CSG) included equality of opportunity as one of its key principles, and its work was guided by the principle that 'the Scottish Parliament in its operation and its appointments should recognise the need to promote equal opportunities for all'. This has resulted in recommendations which reflect the need for the Scottish Parliament to promote equality of opportunity. For example, the CSG has recommended that the Parliament should sit only in Scottish school term time, that it should meet during normal business hours and it should use clear, simple, gender-neutral language in written and spoken communication.

In addition, to avoid discrimination and promote equal opportunities, the CSG has recommended that the Parliament should mainstream equality. This means that the Parliament should integrate equal

opportunities into all policy development, legislation, implementation, evaluation and review practices. While these processes are the responsibility of every MSP and Civil Servant, the ultimate responsibility for ensuring that the Scottish Parliament meets its obligations in regard to equality of opportunity will lie with the Scottish Executive, and with the Permanent Secretary. The CSG has proposed that the Scottish Executive delegates responsibility to an Equal Opportunities Committee, and that the Permanent Secretary delegates responsibility to an Equality Unit. The Equal Opportunities Committee's role will be to ensure a focus on equal opportunities issues relating to all the Parliament's activities. It will set priorities, monitor progress and determine action. It will scrutinise policy and legislative proposals and implementation for equality impact. (5)

On gender balance in the membership of the Parliament, the Scotland Act is silent. The White Paper states that in terms of electoral arrangements, the Government 'attach great importance to equal opportunities for all - including women, members of ethnic minorities and disabled people'. (6) Individual political parties, however, will be responsible for candidate selection.

The CSG's inclusion of equality of opportunity as one of its key principles and its strong recommendations on a family-friendly sitting pattern, business hours meetings, mainstreaming equality, an equal opportunities committee and unit and use of inclusive and gender-neutral language, strengthen the likelihood that the new Scottish Parliament, in a non-confrontational setting, will have equality at its heart.

Chapter Eighteen:
A New Union Politics

Gerry Hassan

The election of a Labour Government in May 1997 unleashed a fundamental and far-reaching programme of constitutional reform across the United Kingdom. Both a Scottish Parliament and Welsh Assembly were supported in referendums held in September 1997, followed by the Greater London Authority and Mayor and Northern Ireland Good Friday Agreement and Assembly in May 1998.

This whirlwind of activity and constitutional reform across the UK has been conducted with a sense of confidence and statecraft which has impressed and surprised many observers. It is a programme of constitutional change that is more radical than any seen in the United Kingdom in modern democratic times. Its slow, gradual and evolving implementation has been seen by some as a very British kind of revolution, and by others as the forces of the status quo trying to limit and restrict change. Whichever of these interpretations is right, the United Kingdom is slowly defining a new constitutional settlement.

Donald Dewar in a Centre for Scottish Public Policy lecture in May 1998 quoted with approval Professor Peter Hennessey's view of the constitutional reforms that there was 'no precedent since 1688 for such a concentrated and deliberate rebuilding of the constitutional architecture'. (1)

However, within the Government's constitutional programme two areas have been so far left untouched: the English dimension and the political centre of the United Kingdom.

The English Dimension

Labour's attitude to the English dimension has always been more an attempt to accommodate Scottish and Welsh devolution to the interests of the United Kingdom. This was true of the 1970s and it is true today.

Labour's policy on the English dimension covers two distinct and separate areas of policy: the first, regional devolution via some form of directly elected or nominated assemblies, the second, economic development policy via economic development regions. The first policy area of English devolution developed in the opposition years of the 1980s and 1990s spurred on by the example of the Scottish Constitutional Convention and the centralism of the Thatcher-Major Governments. However, as Labour came closer to the prospect of power it slowly began to dilute its commitment to English devolution, firstly, suggesting, any policy would be a rolling one, and then, insisting on popular support via a referendum. (2)

At the 1997 general election, the two strands of Labour policy on English regionalism were self-evident: rolling devolution and regional development agencies. These two policies were even contained in separate sections of the manifesto:

'Demand for directly elected regional government so varies across England that it would be wrong to impose a uniform system. In time we will introduce legislation to allow the people, region by region, to decide in a referendum whether they want directly elected regional government'. (3)

'We will establish one-stop Regional Development Agencies to co-ordinate regional economic development, help small business and encourage inward investment. Many regions are already taking informal steps to this end ..'. (4)

In January 1999 Margaret Beckett, Leader of the House announced that the Committee of the Regions which last met in 1978 would be revived. This will be a committee of the Commons minus Scottish, Welsh and Northern Irish MPs - in effect, an English Grand Committee. (5) There is at the moment uncertainty about whether these proposals will be a block or bolster for plans for English regional assemblies.

A New Second Chamber

The Government's decision to hold a Royal Commission on Lords reform which will look into the roles and functions of a new second chamber (6) offers another way of developing a new relationship between the centre and devolved Parliament and Assemblies. The Government's current thinking is to consider allowing MSPs and members of the Welsh and Northern Ireland Assemblies direct representation into a new second chamber and the power to

scrutinise United Kingdom legislation. According to a Government source:

> 'It would be absolutely right that the whole question of binding the UK together would be uppermost in the minds of a lot of people'. (7)

A new role for a second chamber could have powerful constitutional consequences:

> 'This could help to counteract the centrifugal political forces released by devolution and to give the devolved governments and assemblies a stake in the institutions of the centre'. (8)

Different options in any regional model of a second chamber include whether it should be based on direct or indirect election, and representation by government or devolved assemblies. The German second chamber, the Bundesrat, is often cited as a model to follow and the basis for its representation is the Lander or state government which leaves the German devolved assemblies unrepresented.

The Politics of Asymmetrical Devolution

The Labour Government's programme of constitutional change has invoked language such as 'a rolling programme of devolution' to describe its gradual, evolving and ad hoc manner. At the same time the European Union's political and monetary convergence evokes the vision of a 'multi-speed Europe' and 'variable geometry'. These two processes are actually very similar and the words used to describe one could be used to describe the other. Is the current package of UK constitutional change not one of 'variable geometry' and is the EU process not 'a rolling one'? Both political processes are based on the politics of asymmetrical devolution and development.

UK constitutional change and EU converge influence and interact with each other. This is usually characterised as a one-way relationship by both parties with the United Kingdom Government borrowing on European models of decentralism and the EU idea of subsidiarity to break away from British traditions of centralism. In reality, the UK and EU are engaged in a two-way process whereby the UK model of constitutional change offers a model to the EU of citizen based government that is flexible, open and transparent. It could even offer some practical ideas to the European Union about its future direction - one based more on a citizens' agenda than the federal EU vision of the Franco-German axis.

Devolution in a Unitary State

A unitary state:

> 'built up around one unambiguous political centre which enjoys economic dominance and pursues a more or less undeviating policy of administrative standardisation'. (9)

One of the most common misapprehensions about the United Kingdom is that it is a unitary state. The UK has never had the degree of centralisation and standardisation which is seen in a unitary state, and has always been a multi-national state with different national and local arrangements.

The unitary state perspective has been used by anti-devolutionists such as Tam Dalyell and Enoch Powell to argue that devolution was incompatible with the integrity of the unitary state. Tam Dalyell argued this in a debate on the Scotland Bill in the 1970s:

> 'Would it not be more honest to admit that it is impossible to have an Assembly [for Scotland or Wales] - especially any kind of subordinate Parliament - that is part, though only part, of a unitary state'. (10)

Devolutionists often argued that the history and politics of the United Kingdom was firmly rooted in adaptability and anomalies, therefore Scottish devolution was possible within a unitary state. In fact, Dalyell and Powell were correct in their analysis that devolution was incompatible with a unitary state, but they were wrong about the nature of the United Kingdom.

Devolution in a Union State

A union state:

> 'While administrative standardisation prevails over most of the territory, the consequences of personal union entail the survival in some areas of pre-union rights and institutional infrastructures which preserve some degree of regional autonomy and serve as agencies of indigenous elite recruitment'. (11)

The United Kingdom is a union state where 'pre-union rights' and 'regional autonomy' exist. How else can one explain the 1707 Treaty of Union between Scotland and England which guaranteed the autonomy and distinctiveness of much of Scottish civil society?

According to Michael Keating, a union state is 'a pact' or 'contract' whereby territorial politics and needs can be constantly adapted and renegotiated. In this framework, the process of devolution can be seen as a fundamental renegotiation. (12) A union state is different from that of a federal settlement, as it does not impose a coherent set of rules and arrangements on all regions. Instead, a union state would allow the United Kingdom to develop different solutions for different parts of the UK which were appropriate to their historical background and present-day needs.

The New Institutions of the New Union

a) The Joint Ministerial Committee

The Joint Ministerial Committee (JMC) is likely to be one of the most important forums for negotiating on pan-United Kingdom devolution issues. It was announced by Baroness Ramsay of Cartvale in a House of Lords debate on the Scotland Bill in July 1998:

> *'The Government intend that there should be standing arrangements for the devolved administration to be involved in UK Government at ministerial level when they consider reserved matters which impinge on devolved administrations. It is envisaged that this would be achieved through the establishment of a joint ministerial committee of which the UK Government and the devolved administrations would be members. The joint ministerial committee will be an entirely consultative body, supported by a committee of officials and a joint secretariat ...'. (13)*

The JMC will only envisage representation for the Governments of the devolved bodies and the United Kingdom and will be administered through the Cabinet Office and be guided by an agenda that is shaped by 'fire-fighting' and 'conflict resolution' over issues, and particularly, finances. It will become the main institution where the devolved governments can influence and negotiate with the United Kingdom Government about reserved matters and also be able to discuss devolved matters with other devolved governments. The influence of the Scottish, Welsh and Northern Irish devolved governments will increase in the JMC if they agree on any issue to speak from a common negotiating position, which on a number of issues it will be in their self-interest to adopt.

b) The British-Irish Council

The British-Irish Council (BIC) emerged as a by-product of the Good Friday Agreement as part of a range of inter-governmental institutions linking the governments and nations of the United Kingdom and the Republic of Ireland. While the North-South Ministerial Council had been proposed to appeal to the Northern Irish nationalist community, the BIC was partly devised to offset this and assuage the fears of the unionist community.

The BIC will contain representatives of the British and Irish Governments and the devolved governments of Scotland, Wales and Northern Ireland, as well as English regional assemblies 'if appropriate' and representatives of the Isle of Man and Channel Islands. (14)

The BIC could develop along different lines: governmental, devolved bodies, civic institutions. One example often cited as a model is the Nordic Council which was, unlike the BIC, established as a bottom-up body. It was set up in 1918 as a citizens' forum which took until 1971 to develop into an inter-governmental institution. (15)

The purpose of the BIC is described in the Agreement:

> 'The British-Irish Council will exchange information, discuss, consult and use best endeavours to reach agreement on co-operation on matters of mutual interest within the competence of the relevant Administrations. Suitable issues for early discussion in the BIC could include transport links, agricultural issues, environmental issues, cultural issues, health issues, education issues and approaches to EU issues'. (16)

The Agreement goes on to say in a section which has much relevance for the devolved governments that 'it will be open to two or more members to develop bilateral or multilateral arrangements between them'. (17) This will allow the Scottish, Welsh and Northern Irish governments to use the BIC to develop inter-governmental relationships with each other and perhaps, even common positions vis-a-via the United Kingdom Government. With civic forums planned in all the devolved areas, the BIC could also provide the appropriate framework for developing dialogue and networks

amongst civic institutions in ways which aid understanding and respect of different cultures and traditions in the United Kingdom and Republic of Ireland.

A New Kind of Union

The United Kingdom is developing a new, radical constitutional settlement. However, at the same time as it is embracing the new, it is clinging to the old. Both the 'Scotland's Parliament' White Paper and Human Rights White Paper stressed the doctrine of Parliamentary sovereignty. (18) The Scottish White Paper did so in uncompromising terms:

> 'The UK Parliament is and will remain sovereign in all matters: but as part of the Government's resolve to modernise the British constitution Westminster will be choosing to exercise the sovereignty by devolving legislative responsibilities to a Scottish Parliament without in any way diminishing its own powers. The Government recognise that no UK Parliament can bind its successors'. (19)

The United Kingdom has a firm understanding of how to look both ways at once having for the last 25 years protested that membership of the European Union changed nothing profound about the state of the British constitution. At the same time, Governments continued quietly contributing to the slow erosion of the principle of Parliamentary sovereignty via the enactment of the Single European Act 1986 and Masstricht Treaty 1993.

We will shortly experience a new kind of Westminster rising up out of the realities of the United Kingdom post-devolution. It will be a Commons and Lords where much power and conflict has been drawn away. In relation to Scottish business, there will be no Scottish Question Time, no Scottish Grand Committee, eventually no Scottish Select Committee and probably at some future point, no Secretary of State for Scotland. The profile and influence of Westminster will become less and less in Scotland as we move towards what Tom Nairn has called in his submission to the Scottish Affairs Select Committee 'de facto independence'. (20)

The United Kingdom's asymmetrical devolution may take us into new and uncharted waters and into the process of devolutionary leap-frogging. In Spain and Canada, this has led to the 'lower' autonomy regions attempting to catch up the 'higher' autonomy regions which stimulates them to seek further powers. This dynamic and evolving process can be seen in Spain and Canada with the 'higher' autonomy regions of Catalonia and the Basque Region and Quebec.

A politics of leap-frogging could lead in relation to Scotland to Nairn's 'de facto independence' moving closer to 'de jure independence'. (21) One of the defining areas where conflict and tension will arise between the new devolved governments, English regional development agencies and central government is over competition for inward investment and European funding. There will be a need to set common rules as the Scottish Affairs Select Committee pointed out. (22)

The processes of constitutional change embarked upon by the Labour Government are remaking the United Kingdom and renegotiating Scotland's place in a changing and dynamic Union. The environment that the Scottish Parliament will find itself operating in is one that is filled with vibrancy, diversity and uncertainty on both sides of the border. New institutions such as the Joint Ministerial Committee and British-Irish Council are being created, while old ones are being completely reinvented such as the second chamber.

In the coming years, change will be all about us: the character of Scottish politics will be transformed, the role of the centre will become radically different and more like a referee than a manager, and the relationship between the centre and devolved governments will be founded on new roles and rules. Perhaps, most fundamentally, the very idea of 'Britain' will be radically altered in ways which will make it unrecognisable as it becomes more like the multi-national, multi-cultural set of communities which make up these islands.

Section Four: Reference

Chapter Nineteen: References

Chapter 1 The New Scottish Politics

1. Noreen Burrows, Unfinished Business: The Scotland Act 1998, Modern Law Review, March 1999, forthcoming.

2. H. M. Drucker and Gordon Brown, The Politics of Nationalism and Devolution, London: Longman 1980, p. 129.

3. James G. Kellas, The Scottish Political System, Cambridge: Cambridge University Press 4th edn. 1989, p. 4, 17.

4. Arthur Midwinter, Michael Keating and James Mitchell, Politics and Public Policy in Scotland, Basingstoke: Macmillan 1991, p. 199.

5. Lindsay Paterson, The Autonomy of Modern Scotland, Edinburgh: Edinburgh University Press 1994, pp. 180-182.

6. Lindsay Paterson, Where now for Scottish Autonomy?, Renewal: A Journal of New Labour Politics: The New Scotland Special Issue, Vo. 6 No. 4, 1998.

7. Quoted in Anthony Giddens, The Third Way: The Renewal of Social Democracy, Cambridge: Polity 1998, pp. 50-51.

8. Scottish Office, Shaping Scotland's Parliament: Report of the Consultative Steering Group on Scotland's Parliament, Edinburgh: Stationery Office 1999.

9. The Scotsman, February 5th 1999.

10. Shaping Scotland's Parliament, op. cit., para. 60.

11. Richard Parry, The Scottish Parliament and Social Policy, Scottish Affairs No. 20, Summer 1997, p. 37.

12. ibid, pp. 45-46.

13. James Mitchell, What Could a Scottish Parliament Do?, in Howard Elcock and Michael Keating (eds.), Remaking the Union: Devolution.and British Politics in the 1990s, London: Frank Cass 1998, p. 74.

14. ibid, pp. 75-77.

15. Alice Brown, David McCrone, Lindsay Paterson and Paula Surridge, The Scottish Electorate: The 1997 General Election and Beyond, Basingstoke: Macmillan 1999, pp. 118.

Chapter 2 A Brief History of Scottish Home Rule

1. See Olive and Sydney Checkland, Industry and Ethos: Scotland 1832-1914, Edinburgh: Edinburgh University Press 1984.

2. See T. C. Smout, A Century of the Scottish People 1830-1950, London: Collins 1986, p.248.

3. For a brief history of the Crofters' Party see D.W. Crowley, The Crofters' Party 1885-1892, in the Scottish Historical Review Vol. 35, 1956.

4. For an account of the Mid-Lanark by-election and the subsequent history of the first Scottish Labour Party, see James G. Kellas, The Mid-Lanark By Election and the Scottish Labour Party 1888-1894, in Parliamentary Affairs, Vol.XVIII, 1965.

5. William Ferguson, Scotland 1689 to the Present, Edinburgh: Mercat Press 1984, pp.342-344.

6. Arthur Turner, Scottish Home Rule, Oxford: Basil Blackwell, 1952, p.7.

7. For a detailed insight into the debate around the creation of an independent nationalist party see Scottish Home Rule, the News Sheet of the Scottish Home Rule Association, a complete series of which is held by the National Library of Scotland.

8. For an account of Tom Johnston at the Scottish Office, see Russell Galbraith, Without Quarter, A Biography of Tom Johnston, Edinburgh: Mainstream, 1995, pp.236-252

9. For a succinct account of the Covenant Movement see Robert McLean Labour and Scottish Home Rule Part Two, Broxburn: Scottish Labour Action 1991, pp. 5-11.

10.ibid.

11. Quoted in Jim Sillars, Scotland: the Case for Optimism, Edinburgh: Polygon 1986, p.65.

12. For a detailed anatomy of the 1979 Referendum, see John Bochel, David Denver and Allan Macartney (eds.), The Referendum Experience Scotland 1979, Aberdeen: Aberdeen University Press 1981.

13. The Scotsman, Monday March 3rd 1980.

14. Jim Ross writing in Radical Scotland, December/January 1987/88, pp. 6-7.

15. For an account of Scottish Labour's participation in the Scottish Constitutional Convention, see James Mitchell, The Evolution of Devolution: Labour's Home Rule Strategy in Opposition, in Government and Opposition Vol. 33, No. 4 Autumn 1998, pp.479-496.

Chapter 3 Scotland's Parliament White Paper

1. House of Commons Debate, July 24th 1997, Vol. 298, c.1041.

2. Scotland's Parliament, Cm 3658, Edinburgh: Stationery Office 1997, para 8.7

Chapter 4 The Scotland Bill and Act

1. House of Commons Debate, January 12th 1998, Vol 304, c.19.

Chapter 6 How The Parliament Will Work

1. Scotland's Parliament, Cm 3658, Edinburgh: Stationery Office 1997, para 9.9.

2. ibid. para 12.2.

3. Scottish Office Press Release November 14th 1997.

4. Consultative Steering Group, Discussion Paper No. One, 1998.

5. Paul Evans, Handbook of House of Commons Procedure, London: Vacher and Dod 1997.

6. Scottish Office Press Release July 11th 1997.

7. Bernard Crick and David Millar, To Make the Parliament of Scotland a Model for Democracy, Edinburgh: John Wheatley Centre 1995, p. 1.

8. ibid, p. 2.

9. Scottish Office Press Release July 11th 1997.

10. Scottish Office Press Release October 6th 1997.

Chapter 8 The Scottish Civil Service

1. Graham Leicester and Peter Mackay, Holistic Government: Options for a Devolved Scotland, Edinburgh: Scottish Council Foundation 1998.

2. Scottish Office, Shaping Scotland's Parliament: Report of the Consultatitive Steering Group on Scotland's Parliament, Edinburgh: Stationery Office 1999.

Chapter 9 Financial Arrangements

1. Government Expenditure and Revenue in Scotland 1996-1997, Edinburgh: The Scottish Office 1997.

2. Robert Twigger, The Barnett Formula, London: House of Commons Research Paper 1998.

3. Needs Assessment Study Report, London: HM Treasury 1979.

4. David Heald, Territorial Public Expenditure in the United Kingdom, Public Administration, Summer 1994, Vol. 72 No. 2.

5. Coopers and Lybrand and Pieda, Comparative Study of Local Authority Current Expenditure in Scotland, England and Wales : Report, Edinburgh: Stationery Office 1997.

6. The Scotland Bill : Devolution and Scotland's Parliament, London: House of Commons Library 1998.

7. Modern Public Services for Britain : Investing in Reform: Comprehensive Spending Review : New Public Spending Plans 1999 - 2002, Cm. 4011, London: Stationery Office 1998.

Chapter 10 The Scottish Legal System

1. European legislation is generally incorporated into UK law by Acts of the Westminster Parliament.

2. This is a means of challenging in the courts the way in which decisions are reached by public authorities.

3. Private prosecutions in the criminal courts are also possible, though rare.

4. The Lord Advocate is the senior Law Officer in Scotland. He is a member of the Government, and its chief legal adviser in Scotland.

5. Scotland Act 1998, Section 28.

6. ibid, Schedule 5.

7. ibid, Section 98 and Schedule 6.

8. ibid, Schedule 6.

9. The Judicial Committee is an appeal court which exercises a number of miscellaneous judicial functions. Its membership includes judges from the House of Lords, the Lord Chancellor, and judicial members of the Privy Council.

10. Scotland Act 1998, Schedule 6.

11. In practice, the Lord President of the Court of Session and the Lord Justice-Clerk are nominated by the Prime Minister on the recommendation of the Lord Advocate.

12. Claim of Right 1689, Art 13; Mackay and Esslemont v Lord Advocate 1937 SC 860.

13. The English Act of Settlement 1700, the provisions of which are now contained in the Supreme Court Act 1981, allows English judges to be removed by a resolution of both Houses of Parliament. However, this does not apply to judges in Scotland.

14. Sheriff courts are organised into six sheriffdoms, each of which is divided into sheriff court districts. There are 49 sheriff court districts in total. Each sheriffdom has a Sheriff Principal, who is responsible for the efficient organisation and administration of the courts.

15. The Lord President of the Court of Session and the Lord Justice-Clerk will continue to be nominated by the Prime Minister on the recommendation of the Lord Advocate.

16. Scotland Act 1998, Section 95.

Chapter 11 The New Electoral System

1. Richard Parry, Scottish Political Facts, Edinburgh: T & T Clark 1988, pp. 2-3.

2. Alice Brown, David McCrone, Lindsay Paterson and Paula Surridge, The Scottish Electorate: The 1997 General Election and Beyond, Basingstoke: Macmillan 1999, pp. 139-63.

3. Jeremy Mitchell and Ben Seyd, Fragmentation in the Party and Political Systems, in Robert Hazell (ed.), Constitutional Futures: A History of the Next Ten Years, Oxford: Oxford University Press 1999.

Chapter 12 Relations With Other Public Bodies

1. Report on Non-Departmental Bodies, Cmnd 7797, London: HMSO 1980.

2. Recent books on quangos, which have passing mentions of Scottish bodies but unfortunately no separate chapters on Scottish quangos, include F. Ridley and D. Wilson (eds.), The Quango Debate, Pxford : Pxford University Press, 1995; C. Skelcher, The Appointed State : Quasi-Governmental Organisations and Democracy, Buckingham : Open University Press, 1998; M. V. Flinders and M. J. Smith (eds.), Quangos, Accountability and Reform : The Politics of Quasi-goverment, Basingstoke : Macmillan, 1999.

3. The latest edition is Cabinet Office, Public Bodies 1998, London : Stationery Office.

4. B. W. Hogwood, Regional Administration in Britain since 1979 : trends and explanations, Regional and Federal Studies, Vol. 5, pp 267-291.

5. Scotland's Parliament, Cm. 3658, Edinburgh: Stationery Office 1997, para. 2.10.

6. ibid, para. 6.8.

7. Scottish Office, Shaping Scotland's Parliament: Report of the Consultatitive Steering Group on Scotland's Parliament, Edinburgh: Stationery Office 1999.

8. Scotland's Parliament, op. cit., para. 6.8.

9. ibid, para. 6.10.

10. ibid, para. 2.10.

Chapter 13 The Role of Local Government

1. E. Wood, The Scotland Bill, The Scottish Parliament and Local Government, London: House of Commons Research Paper 1998.

2. The Commission on Local Government and The Scottish Parliament, Consultation Paper One, Edinburgh: The Scottish Office 1998; The Commission on Local Government and The Scottish Parliament, Consultation Paper Two, Edinburgh: The Scottish Office 1998.

3. Scottish Office, Shaping Scotland's Parliament: Report of the Consultative Steering Group on Scotland's Parliament, Edinburgh: Stationery Office 1999.

4. Scotland's Parliament White Paper, Cm. 3658, Edinburgh: The Stationery Office 1997.

Chapter 14 Relations With Westminister

1. Scottish Affairs Select Committee Report , The Operation of Multi-Layer Democracy, HC 460-ii, London: Stationery Office 1998.

2. Procedures Committee Press Notice, January 14th 1999.

3. Robert Hazell, Westminster and Whitehall, in Philip Norton (ed.), The Consequences of Devolution, London: Hansard Society 1998, p. 18.

4. J. A. G. Griffiths and M. Ryle, Parliament: Functions, Practice and Procedure, London: Sweet and Maxwell 1989, p. 6.

5. Greg Power, Reinventing Government, London: Charter 88, 1997.

6. House of Commons Hansard, January 14th 1999, Col. 446.

7. Scottish Affairs Select Committee, op. cit, para. 86.

8. House of Commons Hansard, January 12th 1998, Col. 29.

9. Reform of the House of Lords, Charter 88 Policy Paper 1998, p. 2.

10. Richard Cornes, Intergovernmental Relations in a Devolved United Kingdom: Making Devolution Work, in Robert Hazell (ed.), Constitutional Futures: A History of the Next Ten Years, Oxford: Oxford University Press 1999.

11. Iain MacWhirter, The Bulldogs that didn't bark ... or whatever happened to England?, in Renewal: A Journal of New Labour Politics: The New Scotland Special Issue, Vol. 6 No. 4 1998.

Chapter 15 Relations With The European Union

1. Scottish Affairs Select Committee, The Operation of Multi-Layer Democracy, HC 460-ii, London: Stationery Office 1998, para. 54.

2. ibid, para. 60.

Chapter 17 The Equality Agenda

1. Scotland's Parliament, Scotland's Right, Edinburgh: Scottish Constitutional Convention 1995.

2. Scotland Act 1998, Section 28 (2) (d).

3. ibid, Schedule 5.

4. ibid.

5. Scottish Office, Shaping Scotland's Parliament: Report of the Consultative Steering Group on Scotland's Parliament, Edinburgh: Stationery Office 1999.

6. Scotland's Parliament, Cm. 3658, Edinburgh: Stationery Office 1997, para. 8.5.

Chapter 18 A New Union Politics

1. Quoted in Donald Dewar, Centre for Scottish Public Policy lecture, May 29th 1998, in Bill Jamieson, The Bogus State of Brigadoon: What can save Scotland?, London: Centre for Policy Studies 1998, p. 5.

2. Labour Party, A Choice for England, London: Labour Party 1995: Labour Party, A New Voice for England, London: Labour Party 1996.

3. Labour Party, New Labour: Because Britain deserves better, London: Labour Party 1997, pp. 34-35.

4. ibid, p. 16.

5. The Scotsman, January 15 1999.

6. The Herald, February 9th 1999.

7. The Scotsman, January 6th 1999.

8. Robert Hazell, The New Constitutional Settlement, in Robert Hazell (ed.), Constitutional Futures: A History of the Next Ten Years, Oxford: Oxford University Press 1999, p. 242.

9. Stein Rokkan and Derek Urwin, Introduction, in Rokkan and Urwin (eds.), The Politics of Territorial Identity: Studies in European Regionalism, London: Sage 1982, p. 11.

10. House of Commons Debate Vol. 939, Col 78-79.

11. Rokkan and Urwin, op. cit., p. 11.

12. Michael Keating, What's Wrong with Asymmetrical Government?, in Howard Elcock and Michael Keating (eds.), Remaking the Union: Devolution and British Politics in the 1990s, London: Frank Cass 1998.

13. House of Lords Debate cols. 1488-9.

14. The Agreement, Strand Three, para. 2, Belfast: Northern Ireland Office 1998.

15. The Nordic Council: Lessons for the Council of the Isles, London: Constitution Unit 1998.

16. The Agreement, op. cit., para. 5.

17. ibid, para. 10.

18. Scotland's Parliament, Cm. 3658, Edinburgh: Stationery Office 1997, para. 4.2; Rights Brought Home, Cm. 3782, London: Stationery Office 1997, para. 2.13.

19. Scotland's Parliament, op. cit.

20. Tom Nairn, De Facto Independence, Memorandum submitted to the Scottish Affairs Select Committee, The Operation of Multi-Layer Democracy: Volume Two: Minutes of Evidence, HC 460-ii, London: Stationery Office 1998.

21. ibid, p. 81.

22. Volume One: Report, op. cit., para. 42.

Chapter Twenty:
Glossary of Terms: A Chronological Guide

Gerry Hassan and James Mitchell

1707 Treaty of Union

The union of Scotland and England approved by both Parliaments abolished the kingdoms of the two nations and formed a United Parliament for Great Britain. Scotland, retained many of its distinctive institutions: the church, law and education, and its sense of nationhood.

Post-1707 Independence

Independence means sovereign statehood. It is distinct from devolution and federalism in rejecting a role for London in the government of Scotland. Supporters of Scottish independence have rarely supported autarchy, economic or political isolation (see Independence in Europe).

1880s Home Rule

Home Rule was a term used frequently in the 19th century with reference to debates on the Irish Question and came to be used later that century with regard to similar debates on Scotland's constitutional status. It first came to prominence during Gladstone's famous Midlothian campaign of 1879. A Scottish Home Rule Association (SHRA) was established in 1886 to campaign for a Scottish Parliament and was revived after the First World War. In the inter-war period the term had an ambiguous meaning, sometimes referring to devolution and sometimes to independence. The term was less frequently used in the debates on Scotland's constitutional status in the 1970s, but came back into favour in the late 1980s.

1885 Scottish Office

The Scottish Office was set up in response to a sense that Scottish affairs were being neglected. Over time its administrative functions, budget, ministerial complement and number of civil servants has grown. However, its primary political function has been to represent Scottish interests in government. Acting as a form of field administration, as part of central government operating beyond the centre, it has had some autonomy in the interpretation and implementation of central government policy.

1885 Secretary for Scotland

The modern office of Secretary for Scotland was established in 1885 (though the office had existing for a period after the union of Parliaments in 1707). The office was upgraded in 1926 to a Secretary of State for Scotland, the latter having a higher status. The office is appointed by the Prime Minister. The Scottish Secretary, as the office is commonly known, has sat in the cabinet by convention, war cabinets apart, since 1892. The holder of this office has had the ambiguous and potentially contradictory duties of representing Scotland in the cabinet and the cabinet in Scotland.

1885 Dover House

Dover House is part of Whitehall and is the London headquarters of the Scottish Office. The central importance of Dover House arises from the importance of Westminster and Whitehall in the Government of the United Kingdom. As a member of the cabinet and thereby of cabinet committees and accountable to Parliament at Westminster, the Scottish Secretary requires a base in London.

1886 Home Rule All Round

Home Rule All Round was the policy of the Scottish Home Rule Association (SHRA) founded in 1886. This policy involved each of the constituent nations of the United Kingdom having a domestic legislature. It was, therefore, a symmetrical solution and deliberately designed to meet criticisms that devolution to only one or some parts of the UK would create anomalies. It was often used as a synonym for federalism but was sometimes used as a symmetrical alternative to federalism. Federalism involves the rejection of Parliamentary sovereignty whereas home rule all round involved symmetrical devolution while maintaining Parliamentary sovereignty.

1888 Goschen Formula

The Goschen Formula was named after George Goschen, then Chancellor of the Exchequer who gave Scottish programmes a budget based on 11/80 of the English total. It was never applied to all public expenditure, but was seen in some ways as a forerunner of the Barnett Formula (see separate entry). It was finally abandoned after the second world war.

1888 Scottish Labour Party

After Keir Hardie stood unsuccessfully in the Mid-Lanark by-election, he and others formed the Scottish Labour Party with a commitment to home rule. This merged with the Independent Labour Party in 1893.

1896 Scottish Grand Committee

The Scottish Grand Committee was first set up in 1896 on an experimental basis and was then re-established in 1906 and has existed ever since. It is a committee of the House of Commons and discusses Scottish business though its functions and composition have changed over time. In recent years it has been able to sit in Scotland. However, under the Conservatives it had an Opposition majority and therefore it could not be given much power.

1897 Scottish Trades Union Congress

The Scottish forum of affiliated trade unions separate from the British TUC. Originally formed because the Scots wished to continue to allow Trade Councils to have Congress representation and the TUC wished to prohibit this. It has over the years taken a high profile pro-home rule position, aided Labour back to devolution in the 1970s and acted as a cross-party forum across a range of economic, social and political issues.

1900s Devolution

The idea of devolution has been described by Bogdanor as a 'peculiarly British contribution to politics'. It was first used by Edmund Burke in 1774 in an attempt to reconcile American autonomy with Parliamentary sovereignty, and first entered the British political lexicon at the turn of the 20th century. The term has come to refer to a subordinate (and usually elected) level of government which has some degree of autonomy within the United Kingdom. Different forms of devolution exist but in Scotland the term is generally seen as synonymous with legislative devolution (see separate entries on administrative and legislative devolution).

1924 Scottish National Convention

Formed by the Scottish Home Rule Association (SHRA), the Convention represented a broad range of Scottish opinion which supported home rule. At its second Convention in 1926, it was supported by 29 out of 36 non-Unionist MPs, local councils and the Convention of Scottish Royal Burghs. One of its main aims was to draft a Home Rule Bill which when presented to the Commons in 1927 was talked out at second reading.

1930s Administrative Devolution

Administrative devolution is the term used to describe the territorial departments of central government - the Scottish, Welsh and Northern Ireland Offices. Implicit in the term devolution is the notion that some degree of autonomy has been granted. The term began to appear regularly from the 1930s in Scotland and was deliberately intended to convey the impression that Scotland already had autonomy and did not need a Parliament or Assembly.

1934 Scottish National Party

The Scottish National Party was formed in 1934 by the merger of the National Party of Scotland (set up 1928) and the Scottish Party (formed 1932). The party's original goal was 'the establishment of a parliament in Scotland which shall be the final authority on all Scottish affairs' with Scotland's position in the United Kingdom and British Empire left deliberately unclear. It elected its first MP in a 1945 by-election, but did not win widespread national support until after Winnie Ewing won the Hamilton by-election in 1967.

1937 Committee on Scottish Administration

Committee headed by Sir John Gilmour, an ex-Scottish Secretary which recommended the rationalisation and reorganisation of Scottish administration in Scotland.

1939 St. Andrews House

The growth in functions of the Scottish Office (see separate entry) resulted in a plethora of administrative units responsible for a wide range of matters scattered throughout Edinburgh and loosely co-ordinated. A reorganisation of the Scottish Office in 1939, intended to create a more coherent administrative apparatus, coincided with the opening of a new building - St. Andrews House on Calton Hill in Edinburgh. The term 'St. Andrews House' has been used at various stages since 1939 as a synonym for the Scottish Office in Scotland.

1942 Scottish Convention

Formed by John MacCormick to influence public opinion in favour of a Scottish Parliament. After the war it became the main driving force behind the Scottish National Assembly and National Covenant (see separate entries).

1947 Scottish National Assembly

Set up by the Scottish Convention to develop 'an agreed measure of reform of Scottish Government'. It brought together a range of Scottish representatives - Labour and Unionist MPs, peers and councils who drew up a 'Blueprint for Scotland' calling for a Scottish Parliament.

1948 White Paper on Scottish Affairs

The Labour Government's White Paper was a reaction to the pro-home rule activities of the Scottish National Assembly. It proposed non-controversial Scottish Bills would be dealt with by a Standing Committee and set up a Scottish Economic Conference to aid economic planning.

1949 Scottish National Covenant

Established by the Scottish National Assembly this was a national petition to show the widespread support for home rule. It was signed by two million signatures by 1952 but was unable to convert this passive support into more active support.

1952 Catto Report

Set up by the Attlee Government to assess 'Scotland's economic balance-sheet' it estimated that Scotland was a net beneficiary from UK finances.

1954 Balfour Commission on Scottish Affairs

The Balfour Commission recommended the transfer of several government functions to the Scottish Office including electricity, food and roads and bridges and the importance of acknowledging Scottish distinctiveness in British politics and government.

1957 Scottish Standing Committee

The Scottish Standing Committee was first set up in 1957 to undertake clause-by-clause examination of Bills and vote on clauses and amendments - the committee stage of a Bill.

1961 Toothill Report

Scottish Council Development and Industry (SCDI) report on the Scottish economy. It proposed a new Scottish Development Department.

1968 Declaration of Perth

Ted Heath, Conservative leader at the 1968 Scottish Conservatives conference announced support for devolution and the setting up of a Constitutional Committee under Alec Douglas-Home. This was given the grandiose title of the 'Declaration of Perth'.

1969 Scottish Select Committee

Select Committees scrutinise the work of Government Departments. The Scottish Affairs Committee is largely concerned with scrutinising the Scottish Office and related departments. Like other such committees it has the power to call witnesses, send for papers and records, appoint specialist advisers, meet away from Westminster, and produce reports. It was originally set up in 1969 and worked in the sessions 1969-79 and 1971-72 and was re-constituted in 1979 as part of the Norman St. John Stevas package of Commons Select Committees with a remit 'to examine the expenditure, administration and policy of the Scottish Office and associated public bodies'.

1970s legislative devolution

This term was commonly used in debates in the 1970s to distinguish proposals for a subordinate Parliament or Assembly within the United Kingdom from administrative devolution (see entry on administrative devolution). Legislative devolution involves creating subordinate legislatures - institutions able to make laws - though the composition of the institution might take a number of forms. It might be directly elected by the people within the area or indirectly elected ie: chosen from amongst representatives elected to other bodies such as local government.

1973 Royal Commission on the Constitution

Royal Commission set up by Harold Wilson in 1968, first under the Chairmanship of Lord Crowther-Hunt, then, Lord Kilbrandon, to counter the electoral threat of the SNP and Plaid Cymru in traditional Labour areas. As the Kilbrandon Commission it produced its final report or more accurately, reports in 1973. A majority report recommended a Scottish Assembly elected by proportional representation with the abolition of the Secretary of State for Scotland and reduction in Scotland's Westminster representation. A minority report supported an administrative rather than legislative Assembly and a 'Memorandum of Dissent' proposed English regional devolution. The Labour Party initially opposed the Commission's recommendations.

1975 Our Changing Democracy: Devolution to Scotland and Wales White Paper

The Labour Government White Paper on Scottish and Welsh devolution proposed a Scottish Assembly with little economic powers, no revenue raising powers and override powers for the Secretary of State to veto any Assembly Bill.

1976 Scottish Labour Party (2)

Short lived breakaway party from official Scottish Labour led by Jim Sillars, Labour MP in reaction to the Government's limited proposals on devolution.

1976 Devolution to Scotland and Wales: Supplementary Statement

Labour Government second White Paper on Scottish and Welsh devolution proposed increased powers to the Scottish Assembly such as reducing the override powers of the Secretary of State and control of the Scottish Development Agency, but no financial powers.

1976 Scotland and Wales Bill

A Bill combining Scottish and Welsh devolution gained a second reading in December 1976 only after referendums had been conceded in both nations by the Government. When the Bill became bogged down in committee Michael Foot, Leader of the House tabled a guillotine motion in February 1977 which was lost. This meant the Bill was lost (see Scotland Act 1978).

1977 West Lothian Question

In November 1977, Enoch Powell suggested that 'the West Lothian Question' should be the name given to the conundrum persistently articulated by Tam Dalyell, then MP for West Lothian. The question focuses on the position of MPs at Westminster from devolved parts of the United Kingdom who would be able to vote on all matters retained at Westminster including English domestic affairs. Scottish MPs, for example, would be able to vote on English health matters while equivalent Scottish health matters would be the prerogative of the Scottish Parliament.

1977-78 Barnett Formula

The Barnett Formula is the formula introduced in the late 1970s used to determine changes in levels of identifiable public expenditure (ie: that which the Treasury can identify as being spent in different parts of the UK) in different parts of the UK. Joel Barnett, then Chief Secretary to the Treasury, introduced a new method of determining the changes in public expenditure with devolution thought to be imminent using a formula which it was anticipated would gradually erode Scotland's advantage. The formula was amended after the 1992 general election by Michael Portillo when he was Chief Secretary to the Treasury in an effort to speed up the erosion of Scotland's advantage.

1978 Scotland Act

Separate Bills were introduced for Scotland and Wales in November 1977 after the defeat of the Scotland and Wales Bill (see separate entry). In its committee stage in the Commons in January 1978, George Cunningham moved a Order for the repeal of the Act to be laid before Parliament if the referendum did not get the support of 40% of Scottish electors: the 40% rule. The Scotland Act received Royal Assent on July 31st 1978.

1979 Referendum (1)

Scottish voters voted narrowly for an Assembly: 52:48 but this does not cross the 40% weighted majority (see entry above). Welsh devolution was decisively rejected 4:1 on the same day.

1979 Repeal Order on Scotland Act

Newly elected Conservative Government moved Repeal Order on Scotland Act (see Scotland Act 1978) opposed by a majority of Scottish MPs.

1980 Campaign for a Scottish Assembly

First attempt after 1979 referendum to bring together pro-devolution forces in a cross-party forum with Labour, Liberal and SNP members present. Renamed the Campaign for a Scottish Parliament in 1994.

1987 Doomsday Scenario

Term first invented by the pro-home rule magazine 'Radical Scotland'. Used to denoted the Conservatives winning again at a UK level, while losing in Scotland. Closely connected to the 'no mandate' argument which emphasised that the election of a UK Conservative Government with a minority of Scottish vote.

1988 A Claim of Right for Scotland

Small Constitutional Steering Group of the Campaign for a Scottish Assembly (CSA) under the Chairmanship of Robert Grieve and Secretaryship of Jim Ross. Its report stated that 'Scotland faces a crisis of identity and survival. It is now being governed without consent ...'. and called for the establishment of a cross-party Constitutional Convention to draw up an agreed scheme for a Scottish Parliament.

1988 Independence in Europe

Policy adopted by 1988 SNP conference to emphasise independence as opposed to separatism. This proved a very popular and high profile policy recognising the emerging European dimension to Scottish and UK politics. It was also within the tradition of SNP policy by positioning Scottish self-government in the context of a wider but looser union, such as in the inter-war years with membership of the Empire and dominion status.

1989 Claim of Right Declaration

Declaration signed by all Scotland's Labour MPs (bar Tam Dalyell) and Liberal Democrats at the first meeting of the Scottish Constitution Convention on March 30th 1989 which supported the popular sovereignty of the Scottish people: 'We gathered as the Scottish Constitutional Convention, do hereby acknowledge the sovereign right of the Scottish people to determine the form of Government best suited to their needs'.

1989-95 Scottish Constitutional Convention

Cross-party forum set up by 'A Claim of Right'. Contained representatives of Labour and Liberal Democrat parties (but not Conservatives and SNP), local authorities, trade unions and other bodies. Its first report 'Towards Scotland's Parliament' was published in November 1990. Reconvened after the 1992 election, it established a Scottish Constitutional Commission (1993-94) which looked at areas of difficulty including the Parliament's electoral system, gender and ethnic minority representation and relations with Westminster. The Convention's second and final report 'Scotland's Parliament, Scotland's Right' was produced November 1995.

1989 A Women's Claim of Right

Cross-party group founded to monitor work of the Scottish Constitutional Convention and contribute ideas on women's representation in a Scottish Parliament.

1992 Scotland United
Democracy for Scotland
Common Cause
Coalition for Scottish Democracy

All the above organisations were established in the aftermath of the Conservatives surprise victory in the 1992 general election to campaign and foster ideas for a Scottish Parliament. Scotland United was a cross-party grass roots group formed to break the lack of dialogue between the pro-home rule parties and campaign for a multi-option referendum on Scotland's future. Democracy for Scotland organised the five year vigil outside the Royal High School, Edinburgh for a Parliament. Common Cause brought together a group of pro-home rule activists and thinkers. The Coalition for Scottish Democracy was an STUC sponsored organisation which attempted to break the logjam in discussions between Scotland's main pro-home rule parties.

1992 Scotland Demands Democracy

Democracy Demonstration in Edinburgh in December 1992 at the time of an European Union summit meeting and which attracted over 25,000 people: the largest pro-home rule protest in recent years.

1993 Scotland in the Union: A Partnership for Good White Paper

Government White Paper produced as a result of John Major's commitment during the 1992 general election to 'take stock' of Scottish affairs. Presented as 'the new Unionism' it advocated cosmetic changes to 'improve the visibility of government in Scotland'.

1994 Scottish Labour Party (3)

Scottish Council of the Labour Party renames itself the Scottish Labour Party to emphasise its Scottish credentials and autonomy. Third party to claim the name after Keir Hardie and Jim Sillars (see separate entries).

1994 Scottish Civic Assembly

Set up to compliment the campaign for a Scottish Parliament by widening democratic debate and participation involving national organisations, key sectors and interest groups. It held detailed discussions on various aspects of Scottish policy: employment and training, transport and poverty and inequality.

1997 Scotland Forward

Cross-party pro-home rule organisation set up to win the widest possible support for a Scottish Parliament in the 1997 referendum. It aimed to avoid the mistakes of the 1979 campaign when there was no umbrella 'Yes' campaign, and successfully brought together Labour, SNP, Liberal Democrat and non-party representatives. Chaired by Nigel Smith, a pro-home rule businessman who had been active in the 1979 campaign.

1997 Scotland's Parliament White Paper

The Labour Government's White Paper on Scottish devolution was drawn up in less than three months of Labour coming to power - on July 24th 1997 - drawing on the Scottish Constitutional Convention's final proposals. It envisaged a 129 seat Scottish Parliament with power over most areas of Scottish domestic level, but instead of listing all the powers devolved as the Convention did, it proposed identifying the reserved powers, ie: those which would not be devolved.

1997 Referendum (2)

A two question referendum on Scotland's Parliament and whether it should or should not have tax-varying powers. Unlike the 1979 ballot, this vote was a pre-legislative one held on the proposals of the Government's White Paper, whereas previously it had been a post-legislative vote held after the 1978 Scotland Act received Royal Assent. Also absent this time was any 40% threshold requirement, with the Welsh vote held one week later rather than on the same day. Result gave support to a Parliament by 74.3% to 25.7% and tax-varying powers by 63.5% to 34.5%.

1998 Scotland Act

The second Scotland Act put on the statute book in twenty years. This had little fundamental changes from the broad proposals in the Government's White Paper.

1998 Consultative Steering Group

All-party Consultative Steering Group set up by the Secretary of State for Scotland to consider how the Parliament will operate. In particular, it was asked to propose working methods of the Parliament, rules and procedures and Standing Orders. It also set up five working groups on procedures and Standing Orders, financial issues, information technology, code of conduct and media issues. Main report was published in January 1999.

1999 First Scottish Parliament elections

The first Scottish Parliamentary elections will take place on May 6th 1999 with the Parliament convening for the first time the following week to elect the Presiding Officer (and his/her Deputies) and Scotland's First Minister.

1999 Scottish Civic Forum

A Civic Forum is being established through which many of the myriad groups of civil society can meet, debate and develop ideas and research. While it would be independent of the Parliament it would seek to develop official relations with the Parliament and Executive. Similar Civic Forums are also planned in Northern Ireland and Wales as part of their devolution packages.

Chapter Twenty one:
Suggested Future Reading:

Alice Brown and Gerry Hassan

The list of books, chapters and articles is not intended to be a definitive resource, but to offer recommended further reading in key aspects relating to the future of Scotland.

Background History of Home Rule:

Andrew Marr, The Battle for Scotland, Harmondsworth: Penguin 1992.
James Mitchell, Strategies for Self-Government: The Campaigns for a Scottish Parliament, Edinburgh: Polygon 1996.
Lindsay Paterson, A Diverse Assembly: The Debate on a Scottish Parliament, Edinburgh: Edinburgh University Press 1998.

Recent Debates on Home Rule:

James G. Kellas, The Scottish Constitutional Convention, in Lindsay Paterson and David McCrone (eds.), The Scottish Government Yearbook 1992, Edinburgh: Unit for the Study of Government in Scotland 1992, pp. 50-58.
Peter Lynch, The Scottish Constitutional Convention 1992-95, Scottish Affairs No. 15, Spring 1996, pp. 1-16.
Scotland's Parliament: Fundamentals for a New Scotland Act, London: Constitution Unit 1996.

Scottish Devolution: The Seventies:

John Bochel, David Denver and Allan Macartney (eds.), The Referendum Experience Scotland 1979, Aberdeen: Aberdeen University Press 1981.
Tam Dalyell, Devolution: The End of Britain?, London: Jonathan Cape 1977.

General on Devolution:

Vernon Bogdanor, Devolution, Oxford: Oxford University Press 1979.

General Scottish Political Processes:

Gerry Hassan, The New Scotland, London: Fabian Society 1998.
Jim McCormick and Wendy Alexander, Firm Foundations: Securing the Scottish Parliament, in Stephen Tindale (ed.), The State and the Nations: The Politics of Devolution, London: Institute for Public Policy Research 1996, pp. 99-166.

Elections and Voters:

a) General:

Lynn Bennie, Jack Brand and James Mitchell, How Scotland Votes: Scottish Parties and Elections, Manchester: Manchester University Press 1997.

b) The 1997 General Election:

Alice Brown, David McCrone, Lindsay Paterson and Paula Surridge, The Scottish Electorate: The 1997 General Election and Beyond, Bastingstoke: Macmillan 1999.

c) The 1997 Referendum:

James Mitchell, David Denver, Charles Pattie and Hugh Bochel, The 1997 Devolution Referendum in Scotland, Parliamentary Affairs, Vol. 51 No. 2, 1998, pp. 166-181.
Charles Pattie, David Denver, James Mitchell and Hugh Bochel, The 1997 Scottish Referendum: An Analysis of the Results, Scottish Affairs No. 22, Autumn 1998, pp. 1-15.

Political Parties:

a) The Labour Party:

Gerry Hassan, Caledonian Dreaming: The Challenge to Scottish Labour, in Anne Coddington and Mark Perryman (eds.), The Moderniser's Dilemma: Radical Politics in the Age of Blair, London: Lawrence and Wishart 1998, pp. 111-142 .
Robert McLean, Labour and Scottish Home Rule: Parts One and Two, Broxburn: Scottish Labour Action 1990/1991.

b) The SNP:

James Mitchell, Strategies for Self-Government: The Campaigns for a Scottish Parliament, Edinburgh: Polygon 1996, Ch. 7: The Party Strategy, pp. 172-254.

c) The Conservatives:

James Mitchell, Conservatives and the Union: A Study of Conservative Party Attitudes to Scotland, Edinburgh: Edinburgh University Press 1990.

d) The Liberal Democrats:

Peter Lynch, Third Party Politics in a Four Party System: The Liberal Democrats in Scotland, Scottish Affairs No. 22, Autumn 1998, pp. 16-32.

Scotland: Institutions:

Alice Brown, David McCrone and Lindsay Paterson, Politics and Society in Scotland, Basingstoke: Macmillan 2nd edn. 1998.

Scottish Policy:

Richard Parry, The Scottish Parliament and Social Policy, Scottish Affairs No. 20, Summer 1997, pp. 34-46.
Lindsay Paterson, Scottish Autonomy and the Future of the Welfare State, Scottish Affairs No. 19, Spring 1997, pp. 55-73.

Scottish Identities and Culture:

Neal Ascherson, Games with Shadows, London: Radius 1988.
David McCrone, Understanding Scotland: The Sociology of a Stateless Nation, London: Routledge 1992.
Tom Nairn, Old and New Nationalisms, in Gordon Brown (ed.), The Red Paper on Scotland, Edinburgh: Edinburgh University Student Publication Board 1975.

The British Agenda:

Howard Elcock and Michael Keating (eds.), Remaking the Union: Devolution and British Politics in the 1990s, London: Frank Cass 1998.

Robert Hazell (ed.), Constitutional Futures: A History of the Next Ten Years, Oxford: Oxford University Press 1999.

Comparative Studies:

Michael Keating, Nations against the State: The New Politics of Nationism in Quebec, Catalonia and Scotland, Basingstoke: Macmillan 1996.
Lindsay Paterson, The Autonomy of Modern Scotland, Edinburgh: Edinburgh University Press 1994.